Jim Britt's

Cracking the Rich Code[7]

Inspiring Stories, Insights and Strategies from Entrepreneurs Around the World

STAY IN TOUCH WITH JIM AND KEVIN

www.JimBritt.com
www.JimBrittCoaching.com
www.CrackingTheRichCode.com
www.KevinHarringtom.tv
For daily strategies and insights from top
entrepreneurs, join us at

THE RICH CODE CLUB COMMUNITY

<u>FREE</u>

www.TheRichCodeClub.com
Cracking the Rich Code[7]
Jim Britt
All Rights Reserved
Copyright 2022
J. Britt, Inc.
10556 Combie Road, Suite 6205

Auburn, CA 95602

Jim Britt

Cracking the Rich Code[7]

ISBN:

Co-authors from Around the World

Jim Britt

Kevin Harrington

Tami Lucibello

Carla Martins

Eileen MacDonell

Cornelia Dolmans

Jaxon Smith

Tony Vargas

Michael Bolton

Eric Beschinski

Dr. Steven Greene

Prof. Olga Mroz

Tristan and Melanie Helm

Nicole Odom-Hardnett

Martha Krejci

Dr. Jonathan Glass

Milan Milosevic

Dr. Dennis Reina

Caryn Treister

Joshua I. Gorra

Laurie Cozart

Joseph Nunziata

Susan Welton

Jake Cortez

DEDICATION

Entrepreneurs will change the world. They always have and they always will.

To the entrepreneurial spirit that lives within each of us.

God Bless America and the World!

Foreword by Kevin Harrington

You probably know me as one of the "Sharks" on the hit TV show Shark Tank, where I was an investor in many entrepreneurial ventures.

But my life and business wasn't always like that. I used to be your regular, everyday

guy patching cracked driveways to make money. I had hopes and dreams just like most, yet I worked around people who didn't support my dreams. But you know what? I not only found a way out, but I found a way to my dreams... and so can you.

Now, I wake up every morning excited about my day, and I surround with only the people I want in my life; entrepreneurs who really want something more than just getting by paycheck to paycheck.

Today we hear stories -- mostly from the mainstream media -- everyday about how bad things are, businesses are closing and jobs being lost, interest rates are on the rise, how the gap between rich and poor is growing and how you'll never make it on your own.

But here's what I know for sure. Entrepreneurs are going to change the world. We always have and we always will.

Forget the 1% vs the 99%. 100% of us entrepreneurs need answers. We need solutions. We need something more than what we're being told by those who don't have a clue. We need to start saying Yes! to opportunity and No! to all the noise.

The fact is that it's a new world and a new economy. The "proven" methods of doing business and investing that produced successful results, even two years ago, simply may not work anymore.

If you want to succeed (or even survive) in our new world, you need an entirely new set of skills and information.

You need to "reposition" yourself…often.

You need to revamp how you do business…often.

You need to change how you handle and invest your money…often.

Like any other situation, if you know WHAT to do and WHEN to do it, you'll not only be "safe"... you could easily skyrocket financially.

If you have the right knowledge for today, the right opportunities for today, the right strategies for today and most of all the right character and mindset for today, you can win — and you can win big!

What I've discovered in my over three-decade career as an entrepreneur, is that success in the face of financial adversity boils down to 3 things:

The right knowledge at the right time.

The right opportunities at the right time.

The right you... ALL the time.

The bottom line is this: you can no longer afford to rely on anyone else to navigate your financial future. You have to rely on your "self." The question is... do you have a "self" you can rely on? Unfortunately, when it comes to entrepreneurship and money, many people don't. They don't have the financial education, the mental toughness, the knowledge and the skills to build wealth... especially in an ever-changing marketplace. You need to get RE-educated. You need to REINVENT yourself for success in the new economy. You need to learn new strategies in the areas of business and career, finance and real estate that create wealth or at least financial freedom in today's new world. But that's not all...

Skills and strategies and all that profound new knowledge won't do you one bit of good if you don't have the CHARACTER, the HABITS and the MENTALITY it takes to get rich. If you have internal barriers, your road to success will be slow and full of pain and struggle. It's like driving with one foot on the gas and one foot on the brake and always wondering why you aren't getting anywhere. Your mind is working against you instead of for you.

I have seen business owners come to me with their business ready to go under — and have the next year be their best financial year ever. I've see others that had a business that should skyrocket, yet fail because they didn't have the mental toughness to go the distance. I have seen people stuck in dead-end, dreary jobs break out of their rut, get involved in a brand-new passion, and become wildly successful.

No matter what you do for a living...regardless of your education, level of business experience or current financial status…If you have a burning desire for financial change then you won't want to miss this rare opportunity to learn from the entrepreneurs within this book.

It will provide you with some of the same success strategies that Jim Britt and I have used personally and shared with tens of thousands of people who've had tremendous financial success…people just like you, who wanted to get out of the rat race and enjoy financial freedom.

In addition, you'll learn what others have done, mistakes they made and how you can avoid them. You'll discover strategies that could make your business into a major market leader. I always say, "Just one good idea can change everything."

Success is predictable if you know what determines it. This book offers some valuable tips, knowledge, insights, skill sets, that will challenge you to leap beyond your current comfort level. If you want to strengthen your life, your business and your effectiveness overall, you'll discover a great friend in this book. You'll probably want to recommend it to all your entrepreneurial friends.

Although I haven't followed Jim Britt's career over the last 40 years, but I do know that he is recognized as one of the top thought leaders in the world, helping millions of people create prosperous lives. He has authored 13 books and multiple programs showing people how to understand their hidden abilities to do more, become more and enjoy more in every area of life. I also want to recognize Joel Sauceda, our online business partner. He is the brains behind the many online PR, Marketing, Branding and Lead Generation strategies each entrepreneur coauthor and reader of the book will benefit from.

The principles, concepts and ideas within this book are sometimes simple, but can be profound to a person who is ready for that perfect message at the right time and is willing to take action to change. Maybe for one it's a chapter on leadership or mindset. For the next, it's a chapter on raising capital, or securing a business loan. Each chapter is like opening a surprise empowering gift.

The conclusion to me is an exciting one. You, me and every other human being are shaping our brains and bodies by our attitude, the decisions we make, the intentions we hold and the actions we take daily. Why is it exciting? Because we are in control of all these things and we can change as long as we have the intention, willingness and commitment to look inside, take charge of our lives and make the changes.

I want to congratulate Jim Britt for making this publication series available and for allowing me to write the foreword, a chapter in each book and be involved with the entrepreneurs within this book and series. I honor Jim and the coauthors within this book and the series for the lives they are changing.

As you enter these pages, do so slowly and with an open mind. Savor the wisdom you discover here, and then with interest and curiosity discover what rings true for you, and then take action toward the life you want.

So many people settle for less in life, but I can tell you from my experience that it doesn't have to be that way.

Be prepared…because your life and business, is about to change!

Jim Britt & Kevin Harrington

As co-creators of this book series Jim Britt and Kevin Harrington have devoted their lives to helping others to live a more prosperous, fulfilled and happy life. Over the years they have influenced millions of lives through their coaching, mentoring, business strategies and leading by example. They are committed to never ending self-improvement and an inspiration to all they touch. They are both a true example that all things are possible. If you get a chance to work with Kevin and Jim or becoming a coauthor in a future Cracking the Rich Code book, jump at the chance!

Table of Contents

Foreword by Kevin Harrington v

Jim Britt 1
    Think Like Superman

Kevin Harrington 13
    Becoming A KPI

Tami Lucibello 23
    Through the Door from Victim to Victor

Carla Martins 33
    Women and Leadership – From Good to Legendary

Caryn Treister 45
    Sustaining Joy

Dr. Dennis Reina 55
    The Trustworthy Entrepreneur: A Coaching Guide

Jaxon Smith 69
    The Truth About Habits

Laurie Cozart 81
    Money and Your Legacy: What ripple effect will you create?

Dr. Steven Greene 91
    The Five Structures of Success

Cornelia Dolmans 103
    LIVE THE 5 A's!

Michael Bolton 113
    Becoming a Great Leader - It Starts with Me!

Eileen MacDonell 121
    Stop Editing Who You Are to Serve the World

Nicole Odom-Hardnett 131

Let It Find You!

Tony Vargas 139

Overcoming Victim Mentality to Succeed in Life

Eric Beschinski 147

Saltwater

Jonathan Glass ND, M.Ac. 157

Living Your Purpose Through High Level Health

Prof. Olga Mroz 169

Energy of Life

Tristan and Melanie Helm 179

Rich in Spirit and Truth

Martha Krejci 189

How To Build A Multi-Million Dollar Business From Home Without Ads

Joe Nunziata 197

Elevate Your Energy, Elevate Your Life: 7 Steps to Freedom .....

Jake Cortez

A Vision Gives Pain A Purpose 208

Joshua I. Gorra 219

Maximize EACH Day by Living Each Day to its Full Capacity

Milan Milosevic 227

How Did the College Dropout Who Couldn't Speak English Become 8 Figure Speaker?

Afterword 237

Jim Britt

Jim Britt is an award-winning author of 15 best-selling books and seven #1 International best-sellers. Some of his many titles include Rings of Truth, Do This. Get Rich-For Entrepreneurs, Unleashing Your Authentic Power, The Power of Letting Go, Cracking the Rich Code and The Entrepreneur.

He is an internationally recognized business and life strategist who is highly sought after as a keynote speaker, both online and live, for all audiences.

As an entrepreneur Jim has launched 28 successful business ventures. He has served as a success strategist to over 300 corporations worldwide and was recently named as one of the world's top 50 speakers and top 20 success coaches. He was presented with the "Best of the Best" award out of the top 100 contributors of all time to the Direct Selling industry.

For over four decades Jim has presented seminars throughout the world sharing his success strategies and life enhancing realizations with over 5,000 audiences, totaling almost 2,000,000 people from all walks of life.

Early in his speaking career he was Business partners with the late Jim Rohn for eight years, where Tony Robbins worked under Jim's direction for his first few years in the speaking business.

As a performance strategist, Jim leverages his skills and experience as one of the leading experts in peak performance, entrepreneurship and personal empowerment to produce stellar results. He is pleased to work with small business entrepreneurs, and anyone seeking to remove the blocks that stop their success in any area of their life.

One of Jim's latest programs "Cracking the Rich Code" focuses on the subconscious programs influencing one's relationship with money and their financial success

www.CrackingTheRichCode.com

Think Like Superman

By Jim Britt

"Waking up to your true greatness in life requires letting go of who you imagine yourself to be."
--- Jim Britt

FACT: Becoming a millionaire is easier than it has ever been.

Many people have the notion that it's an impossible task to become a millionaire. Some say, "It's pure luck." Others say, "You have to be born into a rich family." For others, "You'll have to win the Lotto." And for many they say, "Your parents have to help you out a lot." That's the language of the poor.

A single mother with five children says, "I want to believe in what you're saying. However, I'm 45 years old and work long hours at two dead-end jobs. I barely earn enough to get by. What should I do?"

Another man said, "Well, if you work for the government, you cannot expect to become a millionaire. After all, you're on a fixed salary and there's little time for anything else. By the time you get home, you've got to play with the kids, eat dinner, and fall asleep watching TV."

Everyone has a story as to why they could never become a millionaire. But for every story, excuse really, there are other stories OR PEOPLE with worse circumstances, that have become rich.

The truth is that all of us can become as wealthy as we decide to be, and that's a mindset. None of us is excluded from wealth. If you have the desire to receive money, whatever the amount, you have all of the rights to do so like everyone else. There is no limit to how much you can earn for yourself. The only limitations are what you place on yourself.

Money is like the sun. It does not discriminate. It doesn't say, "I will not give light and warmth to this flower, tree, or person because I don't like them." Like the sun, money is abundantly available to all of us who truly believe that it is for us. No one is excluded.

There are, however, some major differences between rich and poor people. Here are some tips for becoming rich.

Change Your Thinking

You have to see the bigger picture. There are opportunities everywhere! The problem is that most people see just trees, when they should be looking at the entire forest. By doing so you will see that there are opportunities everywhere. The possibilities are endless.

You'll also have to go through plenty of <u>self-discovery</u> before you earn your first million. Knowing the truth about yourself isn't always the easiest task. Sometimes, you'll find that you are your biggest enemy—at least some days.

Learn from Millionaires

Most people are surrounded by what I like to call their, "default friends." These friends are acquaintances that we see at the gym, school, work, local happy hour, and other places. We naturally befriend these people because we are all in the same boat financially. However, in most cases, these people aren't millionaires and cannot help you become one either. In fact, if you tell them you are going to become a millionaire, some may even tell you that it's impossible and discourage you from even trying. They'll tell you that you're living in a fantasy world and why you'll never be able to make it happen. Instead, learn from millionaires. Let go of these relationships that pull you down when it comes to your money desires. It's okay to have friends that aren't millionaires. However, only take input from those that have accomplished what you want to accomplish. Hang out with those that will encourage and help you get to the next level. Don't give your raw diamonds to a brick layer to be cut.

Indulge in Wealth

To become wealthy, you must learn about wealth. This means that you'll have to put yourself in situations that you've never been in before.

ON OCCASION, DO SOME OF THESE:

Fly first class and see how it makes you feel.

Eat out at the finest restaurant and don't look at the price.

Take a limo instead of a cab or Uber. Watch how you feel.

Reserve a suite in a first-class hotel.

If you are used to drinking a $20 bottle of wine, go for the $100 and see how it tastes. It does taste different.

All I am saying is, try some of the things that wealthy people do and see how it makes you feel.

Believe it is Possible

If you believe that it is possible to become a millionaire, you can make it happen. However, if you've excluded yourself from this possibility and think and believe that it's for other people, you'll never become a millionaire.

Also, be sure to bless rich people when you can. Haters of money aren't likely to receive any of it either.

Read books that have been written by millionaires. By gaining a well-rounded education about earning large sums of money and staying inspired, you'll be able to learn the wealth secrets of the rich. I just saw a video on LinkedIn with my friend Kevin Harrington from the TV show Shark Tank. He said that one of his new companies just had a million-dollar day on Amazon.

Enlarge Your Service

Your material wealth is the sum of your total contribution to society. Your daily mantra should be, *'How do I deliver more value to more people in less time?'* Then, you'll know that you can always increase your quality and quantity of service. Enlarging your service is also about going the extra mile. When it comes to helping others, you must give it everything you have. You just plant the seeds and nature will take care of the rest.

Seize ALL Opportunities That Make Sense

You cannot say "No" to opportunities and expect to become a millionaire. You must seize every opportunity that has your name on it. It may just be an opportunity to connect with an influential person for no reason. Sometimes the monetary reward will not come immediately, but if you keep planting seeds, eventually you'll grow a fruitful crop. Money is the harvest of the service you provide and sometimes the connections you have. The more seeds you plant, the greater the harvest.

Have an Unstoppable Mindset

Want to know some of what my first mentor shared with me that took me from a broke factory worker, high school dropout, to millionaire?

First, he said, you have to start thinking like a wealthy, unstoppable person. You have to have a wealth mindset. He said that wealthy people think differently. He said, "I want you to start thinking like Superman!" Sounds crazy, right? Well, it's not. It's powerful and here's why. How you think will change your life.

Wealthy people think differently. They really do. And anyone can learn to think like the wealthy.

I'm not talking about positive thinking, Law of Attraction, or motivation. Let's get real. None of that stuff works anyway. Otherwise we would all be rich and happy already. I'm talking about thinking based in quantum physics science. Once you understand and apply it, it will change your life. You will become unstoppable!

If there was any person, fictional or real, whose qualities you could instantly possess, who would that person be? Think about it. Personally, I would say that Superman is the perfect person. Now, you are probably thinking I have lost it right? Just stick with me here. I think you will like what you are about to hear.

Superman is a fictional superhero widely considered to be one of the most famous and popular action hero and an American cultural icon. I remember watching Superman every Saturday morning when I was a kid. I couldn't get enough. He was my hero!

Let's look at Superman's traits:

Superman is indestructible.

He is a man of steel.

He can stop a locomotive in its tracks.

Bullets bounce off him.

He is faster than a speeding bullet.

No one can bring him down.

He can leap tall buildings in a single bound. Great powers to have in this day-and-age, wouldn't you say? What else would you need?

Now, for all you females, don't worry, we have not left you out. There is also a female version of Superman, named Superwoman. She has the same powers as Superman.

Now, this is where it gets interesting. Let's first look at the qualities that Superman possesses that you want to make your own. And to make it simple, I will refer to Superman for the rest of this message, and you can replace with Superwoman if you are female.

Again:

Superman is powerful and fearless.

Superman is virtually indestructible—except for kryptonite of course.

Superman can stop bullets.

Superman has supernatural powers. He can see through walls.

Superman can stop a speeding locomotive.

Superman can stop a bullet.

Superman jumps into immediate action when troubles arise.

Superman can crash through barriers.

Superman can even change clothes in a phone booth in seconds. Not too many of those around anymore. You'll have to duck behind a building to change.

So, you're thinking right now, *'Ok, I know that Superman has incredible supernatural powers, how can that help me? What good will it do me to think I am Superman, a fictional character?'*

Here is where science comes in. This is the part where you will be amazed when you learn about the supernatural powers that you already possess! NO, REALLY!

Your brain makes certain chemicals called neuro peptides. These are literally the molecules of emotion, like love, fear, joy, passion, and so on. These molecules of emotion are not only contained in your brain they actually circulate throughout your cellular structure. They send out a signal, a frequency much like a radio station sending out a signal. For example, you tune to 92.5 and you get jazz. Tune to 99.6 and you get rock. And if you are just one decimal off, you get static. The difference is that your signal goes both ways. You are a sender and a receiver.

You put out a signal, a mindset, of confidence about your financial success and people, circumstances, and opportunities show up to support your success. When you put out a signal of doubt and uncertainty and you receive support for your doubt and uncertainty. You've been around someone that you didn't trust, or you felt less than positive just being in their presence, right? You have also been around people that inspire you. That's what I'm talking about. You are projecting a frequency, looking to resonate with the frequency you are transmitting.

Anyway, the amazing part about these cells of emotion is that they are intelligent. They are thinking cells. These cells are constantly eavesdropping on the conversation that you are having with yourself. That's right. They are listening to you! And others are listening to your cells as well. Others feel what you feel when they are around you.

Your unconscious mind, your cells, are listening in, waiting to adjust your behavior based on what they hear from you, their master. So just imagine what would happen if you started to think like Superman…or like a millionaire.

Here are some of the thoughts you might have during the day:

"The challenges I face day today are easily overcome, after all I am Superman."

"I am indestructible."

"I have incredible strength."

"Nothing can stop me.....NOTHING."

"I have supernatural powers and can overcome anything."

"I can accomplish anything I want when I put my mind to it."

"I can break through any barrier."

"I can and I will do whatever it takes to accomplish my goal."

"I fear nothing."

The trillions of thinking cells in your body and brain listen, and they create exactly what you tell them to create. Their mission is to complete the picture of the you they see and hear when you talk to them. They must obey. It's their job!

Since you are Superman, you cannot fail. Why? Your thinking cells are now sending out the right signal, because you told them to. They are making you stronger, more successful, everyday! You have the ability to fight off all negativity, doubt, fear, and worry—nothing can stop you!

Superman has total confidence. So, your cells of emotion relating to confidence will now create more neuro peptide chemicals to promote feelings of power and confidence that others will feel in your presence.

Superman is fearless. So, your cells of emotion relating to fear will now create more neuro peptide chemicals to create feelings of courage. You are unstoppable!

And here's the key. Others will respond to you in the same way that you are talking to yourself.

If you are confident, others will have confidence in you.

You have thousands of thoughts every day. Make sure your thoughts are leading you in the direction you want to go. Make sure you are telling your cells a success story, and not a 'woe is me' story.

Most have been conditioned to think that creating wealth is difficult, or that it's only for the lucky few. What do you believe? It doesn't cost you any more to think like Superman; and it's much more inspiring!

Mediocrity cannot be an option if you decide to be wealthy and think like Superman.

Your decision, and communication with your cells, creates a mindset; that mindset influences how you show up.

None of that old type of thinking matters anymore…after all, you are Superman, and you can accomplish anything.

If you want wealth, you have to stretch yourself. You have to do the things that unsuccessful people are not willing to do. You have to say "yes" to opportunity, then figure out how to get the job done.

Maybe you are uncomfortable selling and asking for money. If that's the case, then learn sales and learn to ask for money every day until you feel comfortable asking for it. You will never have money if you don't learn to ask for it.

I've learned a lot in the past 40+ years as an entrepreneur. I've learned that in order to have more, you have to become more. I've also learned that if you are comfortable, you are not growing. I learned that I couldn't go from a nervous rookie speaker with minimal self-confidence to hosting TV shows and speaking in front of 5,000 people overnight. I simply wasn't ready. I grew into that, one speaking engagement at a time. Every time I finished a speaking engagement, I would ask myself, "How did I do, and how could I do it better?" I still do that today.

And I've learned from the hundreds of thousands of people I've trained, coached, and mentored that none of us can do something we don't believe is possible. It's not going to happen if you're not ready to step out of your comfort zone and stretch yourself.

This has led me to understand the single most important principle of wealth-building, that has meant the difference between poverty and riches for people since humans first traded for pelts.

Are you ready?

Come in just a little closer. Listen up!

Every income level requires a different you, a different mindset! If you think that $10,000 a month is a lot of money, then $100,000 a month will be completely out of reach. If you believe that having $5,000 in the bank would make you rich, then $50,000 won't miraculously appear. You will never earn more money than you believe is "a lot" of money.

What you do as a business is only a small part of becoming rich. In fact, there are thousands, if not tens of thousands, of ways to make money—and lots of it. What I've learned over the years is that, by focusing on who you want to become instead of what you need to do, you're going to multiply your chances of getting rich a hundred-fold.

Ask anyone who's found a way to make a large sum of money legally, and he or she will tell you that it's not hard once you crack the code. And cracking the code starts with you and your mindset. The "code" to which I refer isn't a secret rite or ancient scroll. It's not even a secret. It's a certain way of thinking and believing in which you've trained your mind to see money-making ideas.

That's where you see a need in the marketplace, and you jump on the idea quickly. It might involve creating a new product; or, it may just be teaching others a special technique you've learned. It may even require raising capital to start a company or to market a product or idea on social media.

Don't Hold Back. You Have to Take Action to Change.

Start right now to imagine yourself as already having wealth. How would your life be? How would your day unfold? Start to own your wealth mindset now! The subconscious mind is unable to differentiate between actual fact and mere visualization. So, by imagining that you already have it, you're encouraging your subconscious mind to seek the ways and means to transform your imaginary feelings into the real thing.

Find yourself some mentors. Nobody has all the answers. Surround yourself with people that will support, inspire, and provide you with answers that keep you moving in the right direction. If you truly want to attain wealth, have a thriving business, or reach the top of your game in any endeavor, having a qualified mentor is essential.

Okay, lets come in for a landing ...

It is absolutely essential to have a crystal-clear picture of what you want to accomplish before you begin. If you want to attain wealth, you must learn to operate without fear and with a sharply defined mental image of the outcome you want to attain. This comes from thinking like a wealthy person, (like Superman) making decisions like a wealthy person and being fearless (like Superman) when it comes to stepping out of your comfort zone. Look at the end result as something you're already prepared to do, you just haven't done it yet.

Think about this. Your success is something that you have been preventing; it's not something you have to struggle to make happen. The key is to not let fear, doubt, other people, or mind chatter push your success away. You'll find that the solutions taking you toward your goals will come to you in the most unexpected and sudden ways. You don't need the *perfect* plan first. What you need is a perfectly clear decision about your success, the right mindset, the right mentoring, and the ideal way to get you there will materialize.

The greatest transfer of wealth in the history of the human race is happening right now. Are you positioned to get your share?

Remember, in order to get a different result, you must do something different. In order to do something different you must know something different to do. And in order to know something different, you have to first suspect that your present methods need improving.

THEN, YOU HAVE TO BE WILLING TO DO SOMETHING ABOUT IT.

***

For more information on Jim's work:
www.JimBritt.com
http://JimBrittCoaching.com
www.facebook.com/jimbrittonline
www.linkedin.com/in/jim-britt
For free audio series www.RichCode1.com and
www.RichCode2.com
To find out how to crack the rich code and change your subconscious programming regarding your relationship with money: www.CrackingTheRichCode.com

Kevin Harrington

Kevin Harrington is an original shark from the hit TV show *Shark Tank* and a successful entrepreneur for more than forty years. He's the co-founding board member of the Entrepreneurs' Organization and co-founder of the Electronic Retailing Association. He also invented the infomercial. He helped make "But wait... There's more!" part of our cultural history. He's one of the pioneers behind the *As Seen on TV* brand, has heard more than 50,000 pitches, and launched more than 500 products generating more than $5 Billion in global sales. Twenty of his companies have generated more than $100 million in revenue each. He's also the founder of the *Secrets of Closing the Sale Master Class* inspired by the Master of sales—Zig Ziglar. He's the author of several bestselling books including *Act Now: How I Turn Ideas into Million Dollar Products, Key Person of Influence,* and *Put a Shark in Your Tank.*

Becoming A KPI

By Kevin Harrington

The Key Person of Influence (KPI) in any given industry is the leader. It is the leader of the business world, the leader of automobile dealerships, the leader of selling hats—you name it. In other words, being the KPI means being the go-to person. The crazy thing? Anyone can be a Key Person of Influence. Any entrepreneur can be a KPI, a doctor, a salesperson, anyone. Just follow five steps and you will be well on your way. What comes with being a Key Person of Influence is value, ideally a massive amount of money, and being the leader in your field. The KPI is the person who comes up in conversations when it relates to a certain product, business, company, industry, or field. This is the person others seek out, the go-to person. Being the Key Person of Influence is how I got on *Shark Tank.*

Here's the story: I got a phone call from Mark Burnett's company. Mark Burnett is a television producer. He produced shows like *Survivor* and *The Voice*. His office called to set up an appointment. Mark was starting up a new show and wanted me to go out to Los Angeles to talk business. I was curious as to how Mark Burnett's company found me, and why they reached out for my services. They told me it was because I was a Key Person of Influence. I was all over the internet as a result of everything I was doing. It was 2008, and I had been in the business for 25 years. I had created huge brands. I helped build Tony Little. I helped build Jack Lalanne. I helped build Food Saver. We did the NuWave Oven. We worked with people like George Foreman and countless others. The problem was, everybody knew the brands, which was good for business, but did nothing for my personal brand. Consumers knew about the Food Saver, they knew about Tony Little, and they knew about Jack Lalanne, but not everyone knew I was the guy behind all of these people. Nobody knew me.

At that point, I made a conscious effort to build my brand. I wanted to become the go-to person so I could get the hot products and the phone calls. I helped build Tony Little's business, but everyone called him; they weren't calling me. What's wrong with that picture? Well, for one, I invested millions and millions of dollars of my own capital into Tony Little, and then he got all the phone calls. Shame on me for doing that, right? So, I decided to build my brand, and that's when I came out with my book, *Key Person of Influence*. I promoted myself by doing radio talk shows, TV shows, trade journals, speeches, etc. This is how I got on *Shark Tank*.

If I hadn't met Daniel Priestley, my book could have become *How To Become The Go-To Guy* because that's what I was looking to do, but Daniel very eloquently created this five-step system called the "Key Person of Influence." Realizing we were on to something, we co-authored and launched *Key Person of Influence*. Let's look now at the necessary steps to become a KPI.

Obtaining Customers

In 1984, I started a business of obtaining customers on TV. One evening, I was watching the Discovery Channel and suddenly the channel went dark for about six hours. I then called the cable company just in case there was a problem. They told me there wasn't a problem, that the Discovery Channel was an 18-hour network. That's when the light bulb went off. This was downtime. They put no value on those six down hours. Instead of showing something during this time, bars were put up on the screen. I started thinking about what I could put in place of that downtime, to sell something, obtain customers, and make money. I'm like the Rembrandt TV guy. I created and invented the whole concept of going to TV stations and buying huge blocks of remnant downtime. In all these years of me doing this, no one has challenged the idea that I was the person who did it, created it, and invented 30-minute infomercial blocks.

I was buying big blocks of time. Why? Because I wanted to obtain customers. How do you obtain customers? A lot of ways, but you ultimately have to get some form of media. How does it start? There are two metrics you have to look at when obtaining customers. What does it cost to obtain the customer? That is called the Cost Per Order (CPO). What is your Average Lifetime Revenue Value (ALRV), or Average Order Value (AOV)? The cost to obtain the customer obviously has to be less than the cost you are going to receive in income from the customer. The bottom line in obtaining customers: you have to set up a system. You have to set up testing. You have to set up as many sources for obtaining customers as possible. Even though I was in the TV business, I didn't just get customers through TV. Customers came through TV, radio, the internet, retail stores, international distribution, home shopping channels, etc. The first step is to make a laundry list of every possible resource for attracting these customers.

Today, some people who are into the digital space are basically just getting customers on the internet. Some of the areas I mentioned above have become very expensive. It's tougher to make money on TV. While we started on TV, the cost to get customers has become too high; so we now have made the switch to digital. When you talk about internet, there's many different ways to obtain customers, from Google AdWords to Facebook ads to social media, etc. You can also attain customers with public relations and influencers. You have to decide what works best with your product. The bottom line is a lot of people do not realize they have to be sophisticated, from a business analysis standpoint, to set up a business. You need a marketing plan to obtain customers.

First, focus on two numbers: your Customer Acquisition Cost (CAT) and Average Order Value (AOV). Those numbers have to work. Customer service is crucial in the business world as well. A business can't have bad customer service and retain customers This is especially true in this day-and-age.

Raising Capital

I had a 50-million-dollar-a-year business, making $5 million a year in profit. Feeling confident, I met with seven banks to get some financing. I thought it was going to be easy because I had a very profitable business. Unfortunately, bank after bank after bank turned me down. I had great credit and all of that. The only asset I had was the business. Part of the problem was I didn't know how to approach the banks. I was a young entrepreneur in my twenties. I had no real credibility in the banking world; I was walking in and just showing my numbers from the year before.

So, what did I do to get the capital? Well, I ran into a mentor who was a former bank president, and he said, "Kevin, you went about it all wrong. I come from the banking business, and if you walked into my office and said, 'I need 5 million bucks,' I would have told you to turn around and get the hell out of my office. What do you have to do? You have to sell them on the future. What you did last year is well and good, but they are giving you money because they know that you are still going to be in business three years from now repaying their loans. You need projections. You need your forward business plan. You need your five-year master plan. You need to talk the talk and walk the walk, otherwise they aren't even interested."

I hired my mentor as a consultant to the company. I brought him in on the ground floor as part of my dream team. To make a long story short, we went back to re-pitch some of the same banks. We didn't get 5 million dollars, but we got a 3-million-dollar line of credit. It was all in how we talked to the banks. We had the same business, but it was all in the presentation. It's all in how you talk and how prepared you are. Raising capital is mental. It's in the pitch. It's in the relationships you build, etc.

One of the biggest challenges with any business is having enough capital to do the things you want to do. You have to have a successful business plan if you want to raise money. Here are the elements of a successful business plan.

> (1) You need an executive summary (one page summarizing the whole plan). You need an industry overview, defining the problem you are solving and an overview of the market.
> (2) You need a description of your product or the service. How does it serve as a solution?
> (3) You need a competitive analysis. What/who is your competition?
> (4) You need a sales and marketing plan.
> (5) You need to identify your target customer and proof for your concept.
> (6) What is your method of operations?
> (7) Who's on your management team, your board of advisers, your dream team?
> (8) What are your financial projections?
> (9) You need to outline your risk analysis and appendix.

If you are going to raise capital, you don't just talk to an investor. I get people all the time that come to me saying they have an idea, and boom… it's on a napkin. They tell me that they just need $100K for 10 percent. I ask if they can send me their business plan. They then ask me what I mean when I say, 'business plan.' If they don't have one, that means I am going to end up giving them 100K and never see it again.

One of the most important parts of raising capital is coming up with a reasonable ask, and then explaining how the proceeds will be used. Many entrepreneurs don't understand this. For example, a guy came on *Shark Tank* saying he needed 150K for 10 percent of his company. I asked what he was going to use the 150K for?

His response was essentially this, "Well, I am going to use the money as a down payment for a piece of real estate where we are going to build a building, then launch the business."

"Okay, so you are going to build the building and then equip the building with furniture. Where is that money going to come from?" I asked. He said once he got the real estate, then they would figure out that batch of money at that time. I told him, "$150K dollars doesn't get you in business. $150K dollars gets you a piece of land. How are you going to build the business, generate revenue, and pay me back?" This guy told me he thought I would have more money for him after that. I said, "Well, no. You are not going to get the first batch of money based on the answers you are giving me."

Instead, he should have said he was going to lease a small office and start generating massive amounts of revenue with the money I gave them. Then, pay me back all of my money, plus a huge return on my investment, and then build it into a global business. That's what I wanted to hear. I want to know that people have a successful business plan, a successful marketing plan, and then I will talk about how to go about raising the capital, how to call on investors, and what the sweet spots are for the investors.

The bottom line on raising capital is, you can't just go build yourself a huge global business without thinking about how you're going to finance it. In the old days, I thought if I built a successful business, money was going to be easy. It's not, unless you know how to do it.

There's an art to raising capital. Part of it involves making sure you are prepared and know how to pitch your business properly.

The Perfect Pitch

While the actual product or service you are trying to sell is a critical part of the process, it is just as important to sell the customer on yourself, your services, and your business. Even though I have made thousands upon thousands of pitches, have spoken to thousands of people, and have seen a great amount of success, I still pitch myself and my businesses. No matter who you are, or what you do, you have to be ready to drop the perfect pitch. It doesn't matter if you are going to make this perfect pitch in front of a crowd of thousands, or a crowd of one. To help with the concept of a perfect pitch, I have created a 10-step system.

Before you can start perfecting the perfect pitch, you have to ask yourself a couple of questions. What are you pitching? In other words, what product, business, or service are you trying to sell? Next, what do you want to get out of this pitch? More customers? More sales? Nonetheless, these questions are for you to answer, and you need to answer them before devising your perfect pitch. The perfect pitch can be broken down into these 10 steps:

(1) The **Tease** is your hook; the period of time when you plant the seed. This is when you reveal a problem. You have to explain to your customers why you are giving the pitch. You also have to use showmanship, which sets the pace for the rest of the pitch. If your showmanship skills are demonstrated in the Tease portion of your pitch, then you will have your audience (or your customer) hooked from the very beginning.

(2) Next up is **Please**. In this part of the perfect pitch, you are telling your customer how your product or service can solve the problem you mapped out in the first step. Ideally, your product or service will solve this stated problem in the most efficient, elegant, and cost-effective way. You have to relay to your customer that your solution is the best solution, and it will solve the problem better than anything (or anyone) else. It is important to also show off your features and benefits, and to display the magical transformation that will take place.

(3) The third step to the perfect pitch is **Demonstration/Multi-functionality**. First, you have to ask yourself if you can demonstrate your product, your service and your value. This is the key to any successful pitch, and it brings multi-functionality to the forefront. It shows it off. Think of this step as an added value. Ideally, your service or product is multifunctional. If you can show this off to your customer, then you just brought bonus points to the table.

(4) But Wait There's More! is the fourth step, and it's not just for infomercials on TV. This is the step where you give more value to your product or service by showing and adding more to the pitch—maybe added bonus items or "buy 2 get 1 free if you act now" incentives. At this point, your customer should already be biting, but now is the time to really win them over. So, show them what else you have to offer.

(5) Testimonials are the fifth step to creating the perfect pitch. You are now using someone else to do the pitching. In other words, who says so besides you? This is the proof behind your business, product, or service. Testimonials can include consumers (actual users of the product or service), professionals (leaders in your industry), editorial (articles, experts, press, journals, trade publications, magazines, newspapers), etc. Testimonials can also feature celebrities. Celebrity testimonials can be very powerful for the simple fact that people love celebrities. Then there are documented testimonials, which can include clinical studies, labs tests, and science. Once again, this is one of the most important areas for creating the perfect pitch.

(6) Another important step is **Research and Competitive Analysis**. For this step, you should be asking yourself if you have done your research. If so, then this is the portion of the perfect pitch when you show off all of that information. This can include information on the industry, market and competitors. It can also be facts, figures, and statistics. This research should show off the fact that you, your company, and your product/service is unique.

(7) The seventh step is **Your Team.** In this step, you are bringing the credibility of your team and putting it right there on the metaphorical table. Who makes up your team? It could be advisers, management, directors, and strategic partners. Your team will help scale, open connections, add on the knowledge factor, and so much more.

(8) Why? is the eighth step. Why are you pitching? How will the person in front of you help? This step will change based on who you are actually pitching to. For example, if you are looking for funds, then this is a big section, and you need to incorporate many talking points.

(9) The ninth step is **Marketing Plan.** You have done your pitch and given out all your information. Now, how will you make everything happen? For instance, you need to know your marketing and distribution plan. As is the case throughout your entire pitch, it is essential that you show confidence. Sell whoever you are pitching on your product or service, and yourself as well. People invest in people all the time.

(10) The 10th and final step is **Seize**. You laid everything out, now ask! What are you trying to accomplish? Ask it! Being the final step, this is the time to present the final call to action.

Remember, each pitch will be different. Some pitches last for over an hour and others last only a few seconds or minutes. It just depends on how much time you are given or how much time you need. That is why you need to craft your pitches accordingly. Practice, practice, and more practice.

***

To contact Kevin:

www.KevinHarrington.tv

Tami Lucibello

My life used to look very different than it does now. As a former corporate employee and small business owner, I understand the agony of being a slave to the clock and building someone else's dream while my own is continually put on the back burner! I am passionate about helping people change their lives for the better by educating them on how to build a balanced life and a successful business.

Over the years I have been fortunate to connect with some stellar mentors and coaches who have turbocharged my personal growth. I've built a business that spans the globe—a business that provides me the time and money freedom to enjoy the most important people in my life. And it's a business that has given me the ability to impact many lives and give back.

I am proactive, advocating for the freedom to create a life by design versus a life by default. I am a champion for underdogs and every-day-people who truly want to create outrageous success and freedom for themselves but might not see the path or have the confidence to step out and follow a dream. I can be that champion because I once held that limitation. I have walked through the DOOR from VICTIM to VICTOR and it has allowed me to go places I could never have gone otherwise. You too have the potential to create exactly what you choose in life! What will you act on today?

Through the Door from Victim to Victor

By Tami Lucibello

"I AM: two of the most powerful words, for what you put after them shapes your reality." –Bevan Lee

Have you ever looked at someone else and thought, *I wish I was more like them? I wish I had their talent, their personality, their house, their money, their figure or build, etc. If only I was better, or different, than I am, then I could accomplish something really great!*

It's so easy to wish we were more like someone else, isn't it? I know I've fallen into this mindset many times myself. But comparison is a thief that steals our peace, our joy, and even our ability to do what we are called to do here on earth. In order to experience ultimate fulfillment in life and make a difference in the lives of others, it is important to discover and embrace the talents and gifts that make you unique. To do this, you must make a conscious choice to feed your mind with what best serves you in order to move forward and become all that you were meant to be. It's easy to get stuck in the wrong story. Thankfully, there's hope and the possibility of beginning to write a new story.

I'm convinced we all have the potential to accomplish something great in life—to be winners. However, success begins with an honest assessment of our mindset. Do you see yourself as a victor, or do you see yourself as a victim? Do you think of yourself as a person who faces and overcomes obstacles? Or do you live hesitantly, unsure and discouraged, believing that all that happens in life is beyond your control—that you are subject to the whims of fate? Every day, in every situation, it's victor or victim—one or the other. It can't be both. Let's unpack these options.

What causes a victim mentality? Typically, it's an event or experience that we allow to steal our power. We have control over our peace, our joy, and how we use our abilities, but when someone hurts us or a circumstance wounds us, it can steer the story of our life in a direction marked with failure and pain if we let it. Let's be clear: it's alright to feel hurt or experience something difficult that makes an impact on us. It's not alright to let our minds replay the story over and over for the next five, fifteen, or thirty years. By getting stuck in a 'poor me' circle of thought, we feed the victim mentality. A victim blames and complains, believing they have no choice. The same inhibiting stories eventually become your reality and you find yourself trapped in a hamster wheel of misery and discouragement. The roots of your painful story end up planted so deeply that you actually believe nothing can be done to change it.

People shackled to a victim mindset tend to grumble and come down hard on others. However, instead of blaming others and wishing for a change in circumstances, what we really need is a new perspective. We need to walk through a DOOR that offers freedom from the spiral of pain in our inner narrative. I like to think of this as an acrostic: letting go of **D**isappointments, **O**utcomes, **O**ffenses, and **R**egrets. We all have them.

D - **D**isappointments we encounter in life

O - **O**utcomes we cannot control

O - **O**ffenses we cannot get over

R - **R**egrets about missed opportunities we cannot get back

Many of us slide into victim thinking through a series of relatively small negative experiences. A single, standalone occurrence won't put us off track, but the cumulative effect makes positive forward progress seem impossible. Some people even what seem to be insurmountable odds from the outset, yet they flourish, avoiding a victim mindset, and in fact, finding a pathway to victory. Consider the story of one of the greatest victors of our time. What if I told you to choose a victor mentality, but you were given no arms or legs to do this? Picture what your life would look like and how you would get through a busy day without the ability to care for your most basic needs. How would you do your job or even embrace your loved ones?

Nicholas Vujicic was born in 1982 in Australia without arms and legs. There was no medical explanation or prenatal indication to warn the Vujicic family of what they would face. His parents and family were destined to confront an outcome over which they had no control. Growing up, Nick struggled with depression and felt alone. He questioned the purpose of his life and why he was born so different from all the other kids. He worried that he would be a burden to those he loved. His circumstances were a perfect invitation to a victim mentality. Truthfully, no one would have blamed him.

In spite of his circumstances, Nick chose peace and joy, and flowing out of a deep personal faith, focused on using the abilities he had been given to contribute to those he encountered. Nick explains in his own words:

I was born without any limbs, but I am not constrained by my circumstances. I travel the world encouraging millions of people to overcome adversity with faith, hope, love, and courage so that they may pursue their dreams… Often, we feel life is unfair. Hard times and tough circumstances can trigger self-doubt and despair. I understand that well. But the Bible says, "Consider it pure joy, whenever you face trials of any kinds." That is a lesson I struggled many years to learn. I eventually figured it out, and through my experiences I can help you see that most of the hardships we face provide us with opportunities to discover who we are meant to be and what we can share of our gifts to benefit others. (Vujicic, 2012)[1]

Nick credits the victory over his limitations, as well as his strength and inspiration, to his faith and hope in God. He exudes an attitude of joyful endurance. Nick refused to allow his physical condition to place limits on his lifestyle. He pursued his purpose and passion for life because he chose not to succumb to a victim mentality. Today Nick's life is better than he could have ever dreamed. His journey of peace and fulfillment began with his mindset. Even though he was given no choice when he was born without arms or legs, he did have a choice to walk through the DOOR that would free him from a victim mindset.

There are certainly people like Nick who have not allowed their circumstances to lead them into victimhood. The fact is, we all have a choice. No matter how you were raised, where you grew up, or what you have been through, you have the opportunity to choose the lens through which you view life. A negative thinker sees a

---

[1] Vujicic, Nick. 2012. *Life Without Limits: Inspiration for a Ridiculously Good Life.* New York: The Crown Publishing Group. Kindle.

difficulty in every opportunity. A positive thinker sees an opportunity in every difficulty. From the moment you wake up, your frame of mind leads you on a positive or negative journey. Your emotions, your thoughts, your perceptions, your reactions—each of these feeds your mindset. As Earl Nightingale states, "Whatever we plant in our subconscious mind and nourish with repetition and emotion will one day become reality." Victor or victim, which will it be? The choice is yours.

I like to think of a victor as someone who has chosen to walk through a door God has opened for them. Opponents want to introduce confusion and scramble perspective. If we settle into a victim mentality, anger can take over our emotions; and over time, unresolved anger leads to bitterness. Unsettled bitterness can have physical, emotional, and spiritual consequences. However, when you take on a new perspective and embrace it as your reality, the obstacles you face will no longer be the negative driver of your life.

It is important to view every difficulty as an opportunity. Try saying, "What happened to me is sad, but I am going to move forward, learn from it, and become a better version of myself. I will let this shape my life's story in a positive way." Two people may each handle the same situation very differently. One will choose to use it as an excuse and get stuck, while the other will use it as a springboard forward. One says, "Poor me." The other asks, "What can I learn?" This will lead each of them down two very diverse paths in life. Our past, no matter how hurtful, will inevitably shape our lives, but it should not cause us to make excuses and fail.

We can choose. Will our past be an excuse for failure? This internal dialogue sounds like, "I am the way I am because of him/her/that situation in my past, and I'll never get over it." Or will our past propel us toward joy and peace? This internal dialogue sounds like, "I am the way I am because I know what it feels like to be hurt/mistreated, and I don't want to do that to other people." Our mentality makes all the difference in the world.

Perhaps these are new ideas for you. As life comes your way, adjust your perspective. "But" you may be asking, "how do I get unstuck if I've been reliving the same mental story of failure?" Well, you need a new story. You need to move on, keep walking through the

DOOR I've outlined. Reflect on every pain and failure in your past and put them behind you. To move forward, you need to seek the lesson and begin a new chapter of hope—recreating a story of success, where you are the victor.

How do we achieve a victor mentality? Hope is what allows us to turn the page and begin a new story. Taking on a new perspective can change the perceived problem. Remove yourself from the story while you examine the situation and look for a new perspective. This doesn't necessarily mean you'll avoid pain, but it does mean you can tackle whatever comes along. You can be a victor, a conqueror! After stepping through the DOOR of past circumstances, you can begin a fresh story as you free yourself from the prison of your old one. A favorite Bible verse of mine is Philippians 4:13, "I can do all things through Christ who gives me strength."

Let me share six steps that I hope will help you walk through the DOOR and transition from a victim to a VICTOR mindset.

1. **V- Vitality**. Be a person who lives life to the full. Remain young at heart, energetic, strong, and excited about everything life has to offer. Live with a powerful sense of purpose and a mission to serve others first. Our reason for living should be to love and serve others. Vitality gives us a feeling of success because our actions have meaning. We all want to know that we have a purpose here on earth. Be the person that strives to live, grow, and develop the strength of vitality. This attribute will contribute to genuine happiness and lead to an exuberance for life.

2. **I- Irrepressibility**. Be a person who is unstoppable. To develop a courageous spirit, you have to believe that you have power— power to change and be a better you! Take time to work on you, for you! Don't focus on your fears because they will keep you up at night and paralyze you from unlocking your full potential. Become strong and courageous, impossible to restrain, and believe the best about yourself. What gets you out of bed each morning? What gets you really fired up? Ask yourself how you can be the best servant to humanity, so you leave the world a better place for those that come after you.

Our courage will know many enemies but standing firm against them will lead to victory.

3. **C- Confidence.** Be a person who lives with assurance. Confident people believe they can handle whatever life throws at them. They take more risks which naturally leads to unlocking greater opportunity. These individuals attract people who share their enthusiasm and have similar dreams. Each of us has people in our life who need to hear our story, so be confident and share it. You may not have a microphone, but you can reach someone. You may not have the biggest house in the neighborhood, but you can make it a home full of love and laughter. You may not look like someone on the big screen, but you can exude a memorably inward beauty. Embrace and celebrate who you are and be confident in being uniquely you.

4. **T- Trust.** Be a person that seeks trusting relationships. Strive to be someone others can trust. Trust opens our hearts and lets relationships grow deeper. You can happily live life without many things, but life without trusting relationships is frightening and cheerless. Always assess, develop, and refine the ways you engage with those around you. Have you stopped trusting people because you have encountered someone untrustworthy? Have you pushed away new friendships because old relationships have hurt you? Learning to overcome offenses from the past will lead to victory in your future. People will disappoint you, but you can still learn to trust as you forgive others along your journey. Trust and move forward and you will discover deeper joy.

5. **O- Optimism**. Be a person who chooses a positive perspective. Challenge yourself and others to recognize and appreciate the good around you in spite of undesirable circumstances. Choose contentment. When you share unwavering optimism, you naturally attract like-minded people. Albert Einstein said, "In the middle of every difficulty lies opportunity." In our world the government and media have set us up for victimhood. Others want us to accept this mindset because it helps us forget how strong we really are. Our thoughts have the power to inspire us and set us on a bold and exciting course. What's

more, when your outlook is positive, you can give hope to others. With our words and attitude, we have the power to inspire and change lives in amazing ways.

6. **R- Respect**. Be a person who esteems yourself and others. First, we need to love and accept ourselves. Respect yourself no matter what has happened in your past. We all know people who carry the burden of regret and lose respect for themselves. This affects the way they live. Sometimes, we feel bad because we are not living up to the standard, we know we should. Too many people want to be someone else instead of becoming the best they can be. When you choose to esteem yourself, you will treat your heart, your mind, and your body differently. You will grow to enjoy how you were created. Respecting yourself will keep you from being too hard on yourself and enable you to respect others. Valuing other people for who they are will allow you to express sincere appreciation. It will open up relationships with people who share your mindset and provide positive experiences.

"Cracking the Rich Code" begins with your mindset. Each day, we have a choice.

> "Every test in our life makes us bitter or better, every problem comes to break us or make us. The choice is ours whether we become victim or victor." –Lorenzo Dozier

Something special happens when we set our mindset correctly. As we walk through the DOOR, we can become a VICTOR—choosing vitality, irrepressibility, confidence, trust, optimism, and respect. Living deliberately in light of these six attributes, we begin to believe what we should believe and understand what we really want deep down. Will you take the first step to believe the best? The choices you make today will have a lasting impact on your future, your family, and your blessing in life. Will you live as a victim or a victor?

If you are looking for growth and the opportunity to have more time and money freedom, I'd invite you to join my success team. We can help you build a system that allows you to earn passively. The future is changing. Seize the opportunity to set a new course!

***

To contact Tami:

Tami Lucibello

847-774-0376

tlucibello@gmail.com

www.tamilucibello.com

https://www.facebook.com/tlucibello

https://instagram.com/tamilucibello?utm_medium=copy_link

Carla Martins

Life & Leadership Coach / Mentor / People's Professional.

I am Carla, one of BelightU co-founders. I am a people's professional, a mentor, a Certified Coach and I am here to inspire you to live your best life!

I help women who feel stuck and overwhelmed to unleash their inner power and increase their confidence, self-esteem, performance, and peace of mind.

I have more than 20 years of experience and have helped many people transform their lives. I have been on a long and continuous journey of learning and transformation. Through my life stories, personal and professional experience working with people, and my coaching certification; I have developed the knowledge, skills, tools, and strategies that will facilitate your transformation and growth in all the areas of your life. And most importantly, I learn from my clients, colleagues, and loved ones every day.

My passion and my mission is to help you find the solutions which will allow you to become the best you can be and transform your life.

QUALIFICATIONS AND CREDENTIALS

Certified Life & Success Coach~~Member of the Association for Coaching~~Steps Ahead Mentor~~CIPD Level 7 Diploma in Human Resources Management~~Master's Degree in Management~~MBA in International Management

Women and Leadership – From Good to Legendary

By Carla Martins

For centuries, leadership has been associated with men. As heads of the family, in powerful government positions, dominating in entrepreneurial pursuits as business founders, and in leadership positions in the workplace.

Despite the progress made over the last 25 years, the 2020 United Nations Report - "The World's Women 2020: Trends and Statistics" show that progress on equal rights and equal power is insubstantial.

Some underwhelming highlights from the report include:

- As of 2020, only 47% of women of working age took part in the labour market, compared to 74% of men. Resulting in a 27% gender gap globally.
- In 2019, only 28% of managerial positions were held by women globally. This is almost the same number as back in 1995.
- Only 18% of Chief Executive Officers positions were held by women. Among Fortune 500 corporations, women accounted for just 7.4%.
- As reported back in 2017, women still have less access to formal financial services (65%) compared to men (72%), meaning they're less likely to create their own businesses and fulfil their potential as entrepreneurs.
- As of 2020, women held only 20.5% of high-level legislative positions.

You might be thinking: "governments need to do more"; "companies need to change their policies and practice what they preach"; "education is crucial to change these numbers"; "society needs to adjust and change". Am I right? Those are all valid thoughts and it's obvious that a lot needs to be done for women to have an equal voice and opportunities as men.

This chapter focuses on what **we** as women can do to change these statistics instead of leaving it up to others.

How to become a leader in your personal life and in business

My goal is to provide you with practical guidance that you can apply in your daily life to enhance your leadership abilities so you can live a happier and more fulfilled life. This is informed by years of studying under renowned mentors and experts and practised over the last 20 years.

1. Be self-aware, love yourself and be confident

Research suggests that self-awareness is linked to successful leadership in life and in business. Knowing yourself, your strengths and limitations will help you fill in the gaps necessary to grow as a human being and as a leader. It gives you the ability to move from where you are to where you want to go. To become your best self. Additionally, it'll increase your confidence and self-love. Also important is external self-awareness which is being able to understand how others see you.

Do you know that in research involving 5000 participants, Eurich, T. (2018) found that most people believed that they were self-aware but only 10-15% of their sample were actually self-aware?

Self-confidence is another key trait found in leaders. If you Google the word confidence, you'll get millions of results, but I like Wikipedia's definition best. It's a definition I agree wholeheartedly with - "Confidence comes from the Latin word 'fidere' which means "to trust"; therefore, having self-confidence is to have trust in one's self". Think about it! Having trust in yourself. Feeling happy about your own skills and abilities. Feeling confident and acknowledging your accomplishments. Accepting and having a positive view of yourself.

Just so you know, feeling the kind of confidence I'm talking about, is not arrogance. Arrogance comes from a place of insecurity and ego where someone thinks and feels that they are superior and better than everyone else and needs recognition.

You are confident because you know you're not better than anyone else. You just strive to be better today than you were yesterday.

And please don't' allow others to dictate how you feel about yourself.

Take these key actions to build self-awareness and confidence:

✓ *Learn something new every day*

Action:

Schedule in your calendar:

- A 30 – 60 minutes learning experience: it can be anything from reading a book, listening to a podcast, watching a webinar, participating in or speaking at a conference, talking with an expert, learning a new language to watching a documentary about the mind.

✓ *Mindfulness, self-love and self-care*

We all have busy lives filled with careers, family and social responsibilities so we sometimes neglect self-care – the one practice that keeps us centred, calm and boosts our self-love and confidence. As a mother, entrepreneur and professional, experience has taught me the importance of self-care. Small and simple practices that I've developed over the years helped me become a better human being as well as a better professional and leader. My favourite selfcare practices include mindfulness, meditation, regular walks and connection with nature and travel - yes travel for me is self-care.

A technique that works wonders for me and helps me to centre and be at peace is mindfulness of breath.

Action:

Take moments of breath during the day to connect your mind and body to the present moment.

- Find a comfortable posture (sit in a chair, on a couch, cross-legged on the floor - lean against a wall to make it easier or lie down) and close your eyes.
- Relax and become aware of the sensations of breathing. Just feel that experience.

- When you find yourself thinking don't try to control your thoughts! Let them pass and when you're ready come back to the breath.
- Continue to stay with the breath, without trying to change its depth or speed. Just let the experience be as it is.
- After five or ten minutes, gently open your eyes. You can repeat this exercise whenever you need it.

Another favourite of mine is a home spa.

Action:

Go crazy and prepare your bathroom as if it's a spa. Light scented candles across the bathroom (be careful not to cause a fire!), add a bathtub caddy so you can put your drink (for example an herbal tea or a glass of your favourite wine) and your favourite beauty products. Set the mood with relaxing music, use rich bath salts or essential oils and indulge in a rejuvenating experience.

Always remember that you're unique, loved and deserve to enjoy rituals that take care of you.

✓ ***Celebrate every little win***

Do you celebrate enough? Probably not. Celebrating success is not just about you. I've learned that celebrating every little win and recognising our achievements increases our confidence and self-esteem. It also brings so many additional positive outcomes to us and those around us. If you're a leader who celebrates, your team will thrive.

Action:

How you celebrate is up to you, just do it often and have fun.

2. See your mind as your best friend

One of my mentors, Bob Proctor always says that our mind is powerful, and our conscious mind has powerful resources that we usually ignore. These are our imagination, memory, will, reason, perception and intuition. If you start to use them regularly, you'll notice drastic changes in the paradigms and beliefs in your subconscious mind. This'll help you to thrive and achieve anything you want. Use your consciousness to drive your life and direct it to where you want it to go.

✓ *Visualize*

A simple technique I use to practice this principle is to write down what I want (my goals) as if I've already got it and then visualise it.

Action:

- Imagine that your goal is to have a monthly income of $20,000. You can write something like: "*I am so grateful and happy that my monthly income is $20,000. I am financially abundant, I am healthy, I am wealthy, and it's done*".

- Write your desire daily in your journal, visualize it and feel the emotions associated with it. This simple exercise will help you engrave your desire into your subconscious mind, changing paradigms and programming your subconscious mind to operate on high vibrational frequency which is necessary for you to act and get the results you want.

✓ **Be emotionally agile**

I've learnt with Jay Shetty the O-A-M (Observe, Acknowledge and Move on) technique which in my experience is an effective way to become emotionally agile. Practicing this technique daily shifted the way I respond to my thoughts, emotions and feelings. The purpose is not to control them but peacefully navigate through them. Strong emotions, thoughts and feelings - negative or positive are not good or bad, but a way of revealing something or getting us to act.

Action:

- Whenever you feel stressed, anxious, sad or negative; stop for a few moments and observe with curiosity and self-compassion. Label your thoughts, feelings and emotions, and understand why they are showing up.

- Acknowledge and accept that it's okay to not feel good all the time.
- Finally move on without attaching to or identifying with them. If necessary, respond by taking small steps driven by and aligned with your core values and what you want.

3. Embrace Failure

One of the most important lessons I've learned in life is to embrace failure. Back in 2008, I decided to become an entrepreneur after many years of working in the corporate sector.

I created different businesses with some partners but unfortunately those businesses failed, and I found myself facing bankruptcy.

I saw this as a big failure in life at the time, I was devastated. I couldn't breathe or cry - I felt useless, incompetent, unworthy, and a bad mother.

It affected me as an individual, as a woman, a mother, and a professional, and had a huge impact on my identity and how I saw myself. But while at the bottom, I **stopped to reflect and asked a few questions**.

✓ *If you're feeling like a failure*

Action:

Go deeper into yourself and ask:

- What does success look like to me? Does the fact that something didn't work out mean I'm a failure?
- Do these failures define me as an individual, a woman, or even as a professional?
- What previous successes have I had before these failures? Remember all your accomplishments!
- Does my journey need to be the same as everyone else?
- Do I need to succeed every time in all areas and in all my projects?

Reflecting and answering these questions will help you think for yourself and find the right answers.

Key takeaways from my own experience:

a) Stay true to yourself, **fail fast and fail forward.** If something's not working, acknowledge and course correct quickly.

b) Believe in yourself. Follow your dreams and never give up. If you fail, try again and again.

c) As I've mentioned before, use your thoughts, feelings, and emotions as a vessel of growth rather than destruction. When they arise, it's always important to observe and recognize them, but don't make decisions from them. Move to a different state first - where you feel stronger, positive, and empowered to make the best decisions.

d) Failures don't define you, they're just events. How truthful you are with yourself and others, how you respond to life's events, how you impact other people's lives, how you share love and light in this world, is what defines you.

e) You'll come out of the experience stronger, wiser, more resilient, and determined.

4. Be a Coach to yourself and others

Since a very young age, people have been coming to me for advice and I've always been happy to help. I thought providing advice and solving people's problems was a good thing, but I've come to realise it isn't. It's true that in some situations, providing advice is good but in most cases, it denies the other person the opportunity to think for themselves, to learn and grow.

Developing a coaching mindset requires knowledge and experience, but mostly a sense of responsibility, compassion, wisdom and a desire to help and serve others.

Through coaching, leaders can help those around them to develop self-awareness, to reflect on their own purpose, values and strengths. To think for themselves and design the life they want.

Different academic studies have shown that women are more likely to lead through inspiration and alignment with meaning and purpose, and therefore transform people's attitudes and paradigms.

Let's lead by example and nurture a coaching mindset that drives change in paradigms that don't serve us anymore. Empower people to transform and be the best they can be.

I've developed BelightU 1:1 Coaching Framework to support my coaching and leadership journey both in life and in business. My challenge to you is to try it out.

5. Be Compassionate

I've always resonated with what Jeff Weiner says about compassion; that it's empathy plus action and after following his work on compassionate leadership, I have been applying this principle in my professional and personal life over the last 10 years. I assure you that the impact and transformation is immense.

   ✓ ***Lead with compassion and love***

   Action:

Next time you have a challenging situation:

- Put yourself in the other person shoes, see the world through their eyes and ease their pain by taking action to help them. This'll cultivate trust and strengthen all your relationships, both personal and professional.

6. Create your own leadership journey and inspire

To become a legendary leader, you'll need to move out of your comfort zone and be ready to lead from where you are with conviction and confidence.

<u>Develop and implement the techniques, tips and tools below. Don't be afraid to ask for help. Be courageous. You are not alone in this journey.</u>

   ✓ *Awareness*

I've already mentioned self-awareness as a key trait of a leader. It's also important to be aware of your external environment including those around you in your personal life, your team, your organisation. Even further out, be aware of the marketplace and have global awareness (competitors, political, economic, social, technological, legal and environmental).

Action:

- A useful strategic business tool I'd recommend you use to increase your awareness and knowledge of your external environment is the PESTLE analysis.

✓ ***Clarity of Vision***

Whether in your personal life, as an entrepreneur or a leader in an organisation; having clarity is essential for success.

Action:

- Write your Vision, Mission, Values, Value Proposition, Strategy, Who you serve, Priorities, Objectives/Goals and Success/Performance Measures. This'll help you to get clarity and be laser focused on what you need to do to achieve what you want.

✓ ***Focus***

We usually focus on how we split up our time instead of how we split our energy. We're always multi-tasking and women in particular are proud of being able to do many things at the same time. However, what I've learned over the years is that dividing time between many things can be harmful and can hinder the outcome you want. We should instead invest our time and energy in fewer things at a time and focus on doing them better.

Action:

- First create a daily time log for a week and monitor the time you spend on each activity.
- Review and reflect on the level of time and energy you spend during each activity and the outcomes.
- Then think about spending maximum energy on your most important activities.

✓ ***Communicate to Inspire***

As a leader in life and business, you must communicate the right message and information to the right people at the right time. Legendary leaders have a clear vision and set of values, great belief and conviction in what they are conveying and always believe in inspiring others to achieve their shared objectives.

Being an effective communicator does not mean being a great talker. The key difference is that **effective communicators and legendary leaders possess a unique ability to listen to others**. This makes them good observers and enables them to read their audience (either a person or group) by analysing the behaviours, attitudes, activities, ideals, and anxieties so they're able to adjust their messages to the situation.

Action:

- A useful technique to help you evolve as an effective communicator and inspiring leader is to write down, as suggested above, your personal vision and values as well as your leadership values. If you work for an organisation the next step is to think about how your vision and values align with your organisation.
- Then, make sure that what you do, say, and feel is in alignment with your vision and values. This'll convey authenticity when you're communicating your message.

7. Practice, Practice, Practice

To master anything in life, we need to practice. Life's not only about achieving some goal or getting to a place. It's about the journey, what we learn and how we progress. So, if you want to become a legendary leader just practice.

"You become what you consistently practice. So, practice consistently what you want to become."

Conclusion

I'm obsessed with action, so you'll notice that from start to finish I've suggested several actions steps -something for you to try.

"Words may inspire but only action creates change."— Simon Sinek

You might be asking at this stage, and rightly so, if I have everything I want in my life and if I'm a legendary leader. My answer to both is; I'm on my journey and this journey will only end when I die or maybe not even then, if you believe that there's something after death.

For me, the key is to live this journey fully. To constantly learn, grow and transform into a better human being. I have everything that I want now, and I know what I want for the future. I'm a remarkable leader who's always working towards becoming better so I can help and serve other people better. Every day I endeavour to do and be my best.

If we all do our best and become better leaders in life and in business, we'll make meaningful progress towards equal rights and equal power for women.

As an African proverb says, *"if you want to go fast go alone, if you want to go far, go together."* So, let's embark on this journey together and transform women's leadership and the world. ***Let's do our best to become legendary leaders.***

***

To contact Carla:

Co-Founder BelightU

LinkedIn: https://www.linkedin.com/in/cecmartins/

Website: www.belightu.com

Email: carla@belightu.com

Instagram: https://www.instagram.com/belight.u/

Twitter: https://twitter.com/u_belight

References:

United Nations Statistics Division (2020). *The World's Women 2020 Trends and Statistics*. Available at: https://worlds-women-2020-data-undesa.hub.arcgis.com/ (Accessed: 15 August 2021)

Eurich, T. (2018). *What self-awareness really is (and how to cultivate it)*. Harvard Business Review

Wikipedia (2021). *Confidence*. Available at: https://en.wikipedia.org/wiki/Confidence (Accessed: 10 September 2021)

Caryn Treister

 Caryn Treister has been steeped in the area of women's health and wellness coaching for over 30 years and has positively impacted the life and vitality of hundreds. She has parlayed that depth of knowledge into a successful career as a Transformational Mindset Coach and Motivational Speaker, where she utilizes her years of experience and transformational results, to empower women everywhere.

As the CEO and Founder of Never Settle Life Coaching, Caryn focuses her practice on women who are seeking to rise up to their full potential in life—incorporating a special emphasis with divorced women by using a range of tools and modalities to help them reach their highest and best self through positive thought patterns, passion, and energy.

Certified in NLP and DHE (Design Human Engineering) by Richard Bandler, Caryn embraces her unique talents with NLP to release what is not serving them, create new habits and a new way of being, so they can move on and achieve the life they have always desired.

Sustaining Joy

By Caryn Treister

Think about how happy you'd feel on the vacation of your dreams, receiving a gift you love, or accomplishing a goal that seemed out of reach. What if you could hold onto this feeling, bottle it, and sustain it throughout your life? Would your life change?

Sure, it would! Although, with all the twists and turns, ups and downs, of our busy lives, it's not that easy. Often, it's because we simply don't give joy, an emotion deeply embedded within us, the time it deserves, which causes it to wane all too quickly. Sustaining joy is key to a fulfilling, happy, productive, and peaceful life.

Understand, I'm not suggesting you dismiss all negative feelings. They must be addressed, dealt with, and released when ready. We frequently dwell on the past or on things we can't change. Learning how to sustain joy will help you move beyond excessive worrying, anxiety and pain. Being an NLP Practitioner, I facilitate my clients with a unique way of communicating, visualizing, and releasing what is not serving them. They learn to move forward as I teach them the art of sustaining joy.

Some assume that wealth alone brings joy. Although financial security can contribute, it alone is not what makes joy sustainable. For example, when asked on his deathbed if he regretted anything, billionaire Steve Jobs said that he had little joy in his life. He said pursuing other areas in addition to wealth were important. As a Holistic Transformational Coach, I wholeheartedly agree that we must incorporate joy into our lives to feel fulfilled before we leave this world.

In another example, my client Mary (we'll call her) seemed to have it all; yet she sought me out because she was unhappy. We uncovered that she was harboring anger and resentment that she hadn't even realized were making such a profound impact on her. When she released these pent-up emotions and old patterns of thinking (paradigms), Mary allowed joy to surface and reside in her life. The key was sustaining her newfound joy so she could give joy a permanent residence in her mind.

Too many people go through life not willing to give joy the attention it needs to improve their well-being and quality of life. An important piece of Cracking the Rich Code, so you have no regrets, is sustaining joy—which also opens you up for receiving abundantly. You get to enjoy and appreciate what you have, serve more people, and help yourself and others in the best possible way.

Sustaining your joy starts with praising yourself often for your wins and accomplishments, big or small. When you take the time to do this, you feed your soul with the acknowledgement you need and deserve. Internalizing how well you've done and honoring yourself gives evidence to how important, worthy, and loved you are. I didn't always do this, and my joy suffered. I remember being recognized for an achievement on stage in a former business, and afterwards, instead of savoring the wonderful feeling, I compared myself to others doing better than me. My mind diminished my joy and fulfillment. Looking back, this made me feel less than, not enough, sad, resentful, and withdrawn. Unfortunately, I discovered that this particular response was formed from certain relationships and situations from my early years. I felt victimized in the past, and it affected how I thought of myself in the present.

Unconsciously, my victim mode was interfering with my business, my relationships, my success, and my joy. I made excuses for why I couldn't do things, had low self-esteem, and didn't speak my mind. It wasn't until I overcame and released my way of being that I was able to sustain my joy and be who I am today. Without sustained joy, I was unable to live as courageously and as fruitfully as I desired to be—loving who I was, while fulfilling what my soul wanted me to do. I took my talents and gifts for granted. For example, when I was on a corporate track team in my 40's and won a lot of ribbons, I never acknowledged or took pride in my wins because athletics had always come easy to me. Taking this for granted, and not giving myself credit, was basically robbing myself of joy and causing me to see life through an unfortunate and lackluster view.

Embracing my own self-worth, seeing every day as a blessing, and tapping into the joy I store in my heart has totally turned my life around. I am confident, powerful, courageous, loving, faithful, and peaceful because I know how to sustain my joy. Possessing this knowledge, my passion for helping others bottle up their joy, and showing them how to live their lives to the fullest, is indestructible.

Bottling up your joy starts with being mindful of the joy you already have. To do this, take a few moments to internalize the feeling through heart-mind connection—gratitude in your heart. The more you focus on positive, happy things, the more you strengthen the neural pathways in your brain. Consistently impressing positive words and thoughts into your subconscious mind conditions your brain for the positive things you feed it. When you say or think positive words with enough repetition, you can override your negative feelings faster. According to the National Science Foundation, eighty percent of our thoughts are negative; that's a lot of frowns for you to joyfully turn upside down! With time, focusing on positive thoughts will bring you peace despite your circumstances, allowing you to handle anything that comes along with ease and grace.

Having harmony in five key areas and becoming whole, allowed me to sustain my joy with a sense of security and richness for an amazing life. I want this for you. Below, I've laid out for you these five areas, with an exercise accompanying each.

Health:

Good health brings much joy, if you let it! Having gratitude for your health everyday evokes joy as well as a good attitude for success in your life, welcoming energy and endorphins to boost your mood and release stress. Consciously developing healthy choices and good habits pays in dividends with your health and joy later. I can attest to that. I believe in good health so much that I became a personal trainer and fitness instructor before I was a life coach. So, I understand the value! I am very grateful for the harmony that keeping active has brought to my life. Even if you are not currently exercising, you can start at any age and achieve results. The best part is, you can tailor your fitness or activity level to your lifestyle. It's never too late!

Here are a few suggestions to move, find joy, and improve your mood: hike, bike, swim, nature walk, take a class, lift light weights, jump on a mini trampoline (while watching TV), walk some stairs, turn on your music and dance; simply expend energy!

Joy Activity: One of my favorite things to do is go for a mindfulness walk, staying focused on what's around me to bottle my joy by savoring the feelings of splendor and gratitude. It clears my mind, enabling me to get incredible insight about what I want to write, talk about, or do that day.

<u>Spirituality:</u>

Developing spirituality is so important—understanding there is something bigger than you, a more powerful force that will work with you when you allow it to. With faith, comes a feeling that everything will be okay and that you are not alone. Feeling peace places joy in your heart that you can bottle up. I believe in God; you may call it Higher Power, the Universe, Source. It doesn't matter as long as you believe that it exists.

Joy is different for everyone, and something that makes me feel whole and at peace is being in nature. This was nurtured in me growing up, always living by water—either the ocean, lakes, or ponds.

One of my special moments of feeling incredibly spiritual was kayaking one morning at our camp in Maine on glass-like water. I paddled to the narrows at the end of the lake, surrounded by the beauty of the mountains and natural beaches along the way. When I got there, it was so quiet, yet alive with nature everywhere. There were tall pines with eagles, beaver, salmon, trout, loons, frogs on beautiful flowering lily pads, and if you were lucky, moose. Existing as one with nature brought me warm feelings of comfort, happiness, and calm; and I knew that everything was always going to be okay. In these moments, I bottled up my joy and held it within me. To this day, I use this experience when I feel uncertain or insecure. God provides so much strength when we look for it.

Gratitude is a big part of spirituality—appreciating what you already have and feeling grateful for something that doesn't exist yet. Having faith that it will come true and using sustained joy and imagination, helps you to visualize your dreams and desires as if they were complete. The more you embody the end result (or goal) with sustained joy, the more real it becomes and the more action you take towards achieving it. By using your sustained joy, you can easily raise the vibration needed to manifest (imagining through your vision) your goal.

This past year has been challenging, and I've had to muster up all the joy I could to raise my vibration so I could manifest my deepest desires. Using my bottled-up joy got me through every tough or emotional situation with peace and grace so I could achieve what I set out to do.

There are many ways to be spiritual, and it all starts from the heart by giving, connecting with others, meditating, going within, etc. Exploring spiritual harmony keeps you whole.

Joy Activity: Having a morning routine is a key factor for bringing out your spiritual side. Journaling, visualizing, reading something positive, affirmations, and gratitude are all things I do every day (depending on time). If you do nothing else, write three to ten things every morning you are grateful for and feel them in your heart.

Relationships:

One of the major factors for maintaining a respectful and kind relationship is to understand another's point of view; that way, you can communicate with a higher degree of emotional intelligence. When you see another person's perspective on a deeper level, it is easier to demonstrate compassion and forgiveness, even if you don't condone what they are doing. When you harbor negative feelings, they can take over your mind and control your thinking. Therefore, freeing your mind (which admittedly isn't easy) can bring you peace. Remembering the Bible verse, "Do unto others as you would have them do unto you" goes a long way. With this added perspective, your joy rises and success in your relationships improves.

As an example, when I got divorced, I had to find a way to forgive my ex-husband and stop letting the negative thoughts consume my mind. With Neuro Linguistic Programming, I was able to go within to see other perspectives about him I might not have otherwise thought about, noticing his upbringing, behaviors, patterns, etc. I was able to release and forgive what was not serving me to create a life I love. Everyone was amazed how quickly I recovered; it's because I was willing, consistent, and had the tools to sustain my joy. I use these methods with clients so they can do the same.

Good relationships start with self-care, compassion, and self-love, so you can build a strong core. The more joy you feel, the better you can cope and lead communications with an open heart—speaking your truth. Clearing your mind of negativity and sustaining joy makes coping easy.

Joy Activity: Close your eyes and imagine a scene from your life that is bothering you. Observe the picture from a third-party perspective. What do you notice about the other person and about you? Pay attention to details: facial expressions, reactions, body language, etc. Could you have acted differently, or can you find a way to forgive? What lesson can you move forward with? Now, find a way to make peace so you can allow joy to reside within you and have gratitude.

<u>Finances:</u>

Having harmony in this area can really help to sustain your joy when doing what your soul wants and earning the money you deserve. Whether you have a lot of money or a little, the more gratitude you have for it, the more joy and abundance you receive. Sustaining your joy and appreciation for where you are right now will allow you to stay in this higher vibration. Your financial state gives you the option to have the lifestyle of your choosing, and when you focus on these blessings, brings you much joy.

Reading and learning as much as you can to become financially savvy can boost your joy too. Having financial security enables you to give to others and take care of your loved ones the way you want. Also, if you are starting out in a business, it's a good idea to earn money in other ways too—through passive income or otherwise—so you can save or invest and not feel stressed. Sustaining and feeling rich in joy enhances being rich in wealth and can sweeten your journey all the way.

Finding your superpower will give you joy and enhance your wealth as well. Focus on your strengths, virtues, and doing what you love. Be authentic—there is no one like you and there is no competition because you are truly unique. Here's a great quote from author and research professor Brené Brown, "Authenticity is the daily practice of letting go of who we think we're supposed to be and embracing who we are."

This transformation happened for me when I stopped trying to be who I thought my friends and family expected…the perfect wife, mother, friend, businessperson, etc. I felt stifled and it affected my earnings. Although I did very well in my businesses, I know I could have achieved so much more. Basically, my soul was agitated, confused, and often anxious because the real me was hiding behind a mask and I felt seemingly powerless. I discovered that this was not true. Just like Dorothy in the Wizard of Oz, the power has always been within me. I love helping others unveil this truth.

Joy Activity: Ask yourself these questions, then journal your thoughts, goals, and ideal outcomes for them. Notice the joy you have when doing this. Using your heart/mind connection, imagine or visualize what you want every day and bottle this joy.

What are you really good at?

What do others tell you you're good at?

What part of your business (if you have one) do you like the most?
What do people need that you have a solution for?
What demographic is most lucrative for you?
Who do you have to BE to accomplish what you want?

<u>Mindset:</u>

Having the mindset to have and be joy is the greatest decision you can make. Author, Bruce Lipton, PhD. talks about the science of your brain in his book, *The Biology of Belief.* "Whatever you think about becomes your reality." When I read this, I became a real believer in mindset work. Also, Tony Robbins says, "Whatever you hold in your mind on a consistent basis is exactly what you will experience in your life." So, focusing on joy attracts the good things in your life: abundance, peace, happiness, calm, courage, success, and more, when you embrace this mindset. By training your brain to think of good thoughts first, when a negative thought comes up, you'll shift into gratitude quickly, intentionally bottling your joy and creating the life you dream about living.

For a lot of us, this may not be as easy because we have been conditioned by negative people in our lives. You may have had a parent, teacher, friend, etc. who always breathed the negative side of things into your awareness. Keeping your mindset and energy levels up requires being around positive, forward-thinking people as much as possible. You get to choose your friends, and the energy they give off will help you switch out of negativity and into joy.

The good news, when your joy is sustained within you, you can look at negative circumstances from a neutral standpoint—neither good nor bad. A good mindset means always observing a situation from a point of view of peacefulness. Of course, there will be ups and downs, because life is about polarity. However, by choosing to add and sustain joy, you get to live a life of freedom in your mind, body, and soul.

Positive self-talk is a key mindset too, because so often we beat ourselves up for things beyond our control. Now, when you don't do something the way you wanted to, or someone says something negative to you, or you start comparing yourself to others, you can easily apply the right mindset, with self-love and sustained joy, and move right through it.

Joy Activity: Practice positive affirmations every day that resonate with you. The more you say them out loud, the more they become a part of your subconscious mind and you will BE them. Always have them available for sustained joy.

> I am powerful
> I am enough
> I am compassionate
> I am worthy
> I am peaceful
> I am loving
> I am bold
> I am generous
> I am healthy
> I am joyful

When you have harmony in these five key areas of Health, Relationships, Spirituality, Finances and Mindset, sustained joy will come to you easily. Live a life without regrets, full of joy-filled memories and successes by sustaining joy now. Never settle for anything less!

***

Connect with Caryn

Website: NeverSettleLifeCoaching.com

Email: caryn@NeverSettleLifeCoaching.com

Facebook: facebook.com/caryn.treister/

Linkedin: linkedin.com/in/caryn-treister-21893a8/

Instagram: instagram.com/treistercaryn/

Additional info: workwithcaryn.com

Dr. Dennis Reina

Dr. Dennis Reina, along with his life and business partner, Dr. Michelle Reina, are pioneering, thought leaders on deepening engagement, managing change, developing teams and fostering leadership effectiveness through building and sustaining trust. Dennis helps organizations create high trust environments, especially important during these volatile, uncertain and complex times- where people are heard, understood and align around company values to produce business results.

As an entrepreneur, speaker, consultant, workshop leader and executive coach for over 30 years, Dennis co-founded Reina Trust Building®. The firm specializes in measuring, developing, and restoring workplace trust globally utilizing their suite of proprietary trust assessments that measure trust at the leader, team, organizational & customer levels. Along with Michelle, Dennis co-authored two award-winning, best-selling books, *"Trust and Betrayal in the Workplace, 3rd ed."* and *"Rebuilding Trust in the Workplace."*

Among his awards, the Global Strategic Leadership Award at the World HRD Congress in Mumbai, India and the US Army Chief of Chaplain's award. His clients include, American Express, Ben & Jerry's, Case Western, Dartmouth Hitchcock Medical Center, Harvard, J&J, Johns Hopkins Medical Center, Lincoln Financial, MillerCoors, Qantas, PC Construction, Sandia National Labs, Toyota, US Army and US Treasury, Visa, Voya Financial, Yale and Walt Disney World. The Reina's work has been featured in NY Times, Wall Street Journal, Business Week, Fast Company, Forbes, Fortune, Harvard Management Update, Inc, Time, USA Today, and CNN.

The Trustworthy Entrepreneur: A Coaching Guide

By Dr. Dennis Reina

This chapter is about understanding trust: the pain we feel when it's betrayed and the transformation that occurs when it's renewed. For over 30 years, I've been helping entrepreneurs create, support—and if necessary—rebuild trust within themselves and with others. Here, I'll share what I've learned about relationships in the context of trust building.

More than ever, we need more trust in our workplaces. All business is conducted through relationships and trust is foundational there. It's how we connect meaningfully with others.

It follows that every caring entrepreneur who works with people wants to cultivate trusting relationships with others at work. Reflect on this for a moment and give yourself permission to be completely open and vulnerable. How confident are you that trust is solid in your workplace? Do you see warning signs? If so, how do you respond purposefully?

The Reina Three Dimensions of Trust Model® provides an easy-to-understand framework to help you tackle those questions. It makes trust a measurable thing: giving you the language to discuss underlying issues and take action to maintain healthy levels of trust in your organization…and in your life.

Working with our Model, this chapter gives you:

- Feedback coaching on the specific behaviors of the Three Dimensions of Trust to help you in your business and personal relationships;

- Insightful questions to prompt reflection on how individual behavior contributes to building or breaking trust where you live and work; and

- Supportive tools for identifying behavioral changes you're committing to make to build or strengthen trust in your working and personal relationships.

<u>Dimensions of Trust: The Three Cs® Model</u>

One of first big lessons I received about trust happened in 1972. Newly graduated from college with my Bachelor's degree in Business Administration and my hair down to the middle of my back, I headed West in my Dodge Econoline van…not really with a plan. Someone I met along the way said I ought to check out Yosemite National Park. When I arrived there, my van broke down. It needed a new transmission. The bill was $879. And I only had $80 in traveler's checks in my wallet (in 1972, credit cards were still uncommon).

So, Monday morning, I visited the Personnel Office. I showed them my shiny new Bachelor's degree. They said, "So what, what else do you have?" Digging deep, I shared that:" Well, I was two merit badges away from Eagle Scout before our troop folded." They said: "Good. You're hired. Report to the Mountaineering Center right away."

Within six months, I was managing the Yosemite Mountaineering Shop, learning about rock climbing so I could teach it to others.

I learned quickly about trust—at a deep, visceral level—while suspended 1,000 feet or more in the air. You learn that your climbing partner has your life in their hands. And vice versa. You make the decision to put trust in them and in your work together. That choice—to trust—is at the core of human experience. It's emotionally provocative and foundational to relationships.

That experience laid the groundwork for my professional career. Years later, I began the painstaking work in identifying the Reina Dimensions of Trust—what I call *The Three Cs*®: Trust of Character®, Trust of Communication® and Trust of Capability®.

These three dimensions blazed a pathway for my own healing, building trust and renewal. I'll briefly define these and then expand:

> ➤ **Trust of Character**—act with integrity in all my actions, keep my word and deliver on promises.

> **Trust of Communication**—be truthful in my communications and admit my mistakes when I make them.

> **Trust of Capability**—acknowledge others and myself, and involve them in decisions that affect their jobs and their lives while helping them learn and grow.

To this day, I work hard at remaining true to these values. Unfortunately, we live in a world where it's far too easy to neglect being intentional regarding *who we are* and *how we want to be*. And that diminishes our capacity to grow and learn. We're all prone to living unconsciously and not being fully present. In doing so, we diminish our **capacity for trust**.

The solution: deliberate, trust-building action.

There's no shortcut here. You must achieve and maintain it through visible consistency and alignment between *what you intend to do* and *what you actually do*.

To understand this further, let's look at each one of the Reina Dimensions of Trust in detail.

<u>Trust of Character®</u>

This is the starting point of any relationship at work or in your personal life. Here, your behaviors prove you to be a trustworthy person—someone who can be counted on even in tough situations. Others learn that you're true to your word, that you establish healthy boundaries and expectations, and that you support others as they strive to learn, develop and thrive. This is the most selfless form of trust. It's also the most rewarding when achieved fully.

Let's look at the behaviors contributing to Trust of Character® that are essential to entrepreneurial trustworthiness. **Review the action points and questions below and gain awareness of how you can further build your Trust of Character®.**

Manage Expectations

- Are your expectations understood? Are they being met? Note where you can say Yes and where you say No. Where are they not met? How do you respond?

- Do you understand what others expect from you, and are you meeting those expectations? Note where you can say Yes and where you say No. What might be getting in the way of your expectations not being met?

- How can you clarify expectations and negotiate achievement of them? What implicit (i.e., unwritten, unspoken) expectations need to be made explicit?

- Identify where there's a need to clarify expectations.

Define Boundaries

- Do you have a clear definition of your role and responsibilities, or is there uncertainty? Put yourself in the shoes of others around you. How do your behaviors affect your ability to clearly define roles and responsibilities for others?

- Are there boundaries that need to be established or clarified? If so, what are they and how might that be done?

- Make note of where there's a need for role or boundary clarification. What can you do to clarify?

Delegate Appropriately

- When delegating a project or a task, are the objectives clearly understood? Are there times when you've delegated something beyond an individual's knowledge or competence? If so, how do you manage that?

- Are you prone to micromanaging? If so, what's holding you back from delegating? How do you communicate concerns?

- When delegating responsibilities to someone, do you also give them appropriate authority? If not, why not?

- Identify steps or actions you can take to clarify channels of delegation.

Encourage Mutually Serving Intentions

- Check your intentions. Do you have a self-serving agenda that you've not shared with others? How might others perceive your intentions?

- Which of your intentions do you need to communicate to others? Specifically what do you need to communicate to them? What do you need to ask for?

- Identify areas where your intentions need to be clearly communicated to others. Reflect on where you might strengthen your behavior to support mutually beneficial outcomes.

Honor Your Agreements

- Reflect on agreements you've made. To what extent do you feel your agreements have been honored with others? What about with yourself?

- If you cannot keep an agreement, would others say that you've been unfair: that you unilaterally renegotiated the terms, failed to deliver as promised or made excuses?

- How do you respond when you're unable to keep an agreement? Do you acknowledge your inability to keep an agreement at the earliest possible time, and renegotiate those broken agreements?

- Identify where you need to manage agreements made with others and with yourself. Make a note of where you tend to say Yes, when it may be more realistic to say No. How can you renegotiate where needed?

<u>Be Consistent</u>

- Match words with actions and observe where your behavior is inconsistent. What's behind the inconsistency?
- How do those lapses affect your trustworthiness?
- Make note of what you can do to ensure greater consistency in your behavior.

> ***Reina Trust Tip***
> ***Trust becomes more solidified when our actions match our words and we follow through on our agreements, particularly during period of great change. Words help articulate our expectations, but actions demonstrate our trustworthiness.***

<u>Trust of Communication®</u>

In this second dimension, recognize that trust is built or broken by how open, honest and transparent you are in interacting with others. As you practice this, you become known for speaking the truth and encouraging others to do the same. You become a trusted confidant. People realize you can be trusted to give and share key information and know when it's ethical and appropriate to do this.

As you learn to build Trust of Communication, you no longer engage in gossip or feed the rumor mill. You compassionately raise issues and concerns directly with others You work it out. You start to become the go-to "gut check" in your organization for people at all levels of responsibility.

The behaviors that contribute to Trust of Communication create an environment of transparency and collaboration between individuals, within teams, and across an organization.

Review the action points and questions below and gain awareness of how you can further build your Trust of Communication®.

Share Information

- How is information treated in your workplace? Is it openly shared and willingly provided? Or is it carefully guarded or not shared at all? How can you do more to prevent misunderstandings?

- Do you have the information you need from others, and do they have what they need from you, readily available? How do people access information from you?

- Identify where there's a need to open-up channels of communication with steps you can take to influence that occurring.

Tell the Truth

- Pay careful attention to situations where tough truths are necessary. Why is telling the truth difficult in that case? What's the risk in being forthright? What concerns do you have?

- Are there times where you're inclined to spin the truth? What factors contribute to that? Why do you feel justified?

- Identify the support you need for yourself or to offer to others while revealing the tough truths that need to be said.

Admit Mistakes

- Give permission to yourself—and to others—to admit mistakes. Do you make it safe for others to admit mistakes to you? How do you respond?

- How do you feel when you make a mistake? Do you feel comfortable admitting it?

- In what ways do you take responsibility for your mistakes?

- Consider what you can do to support turning mistakes into opportunities for learning.

Give and Receive Constructive Feedback

- Do this with the intent to support and encourage, not to assign blame. Are you providing constructive feedback to appropriate individuals in a timely manner in support of growth and development?

- Is there feedback you'd like to offer another person that you have not offered? If so, why not? What gets in the way of offering the feedback?

- Are you willing and open to receive feedback from others? How do you tend to respond?

- For those to whom you're giving feedback, consider your approach thoughtfully.
- After others provide you with their constructive feedback, consider how you can best integrate what they've told you.

Maintain Confidentiality

- How are you protecting other people's confidences? Are you able to confront breaches of confidentially with candor, respect and sensitivity?
- Have you breached confidentiality or inadvertently disclosed, proprietary information? If so, what did you gain and lose?
- Identify where you need to skillfully disclose sensitive information in a way that doesn't breach confidence. Consider what approach you'll use and the steps you'll take.

Speak with Good Purpose

- Are you aware of gossip or unfair, indirect criticism about others going on behind someone's back? If so, how do you respond? Do you contribute to it or take an active role in stopping it?

- Do you directly address issues or concerns with the individuals involved? Or, do you use sarcasm, insinuating remarks or slighting digs to convey your thoughts indirectly?

- Reflect on what support you can give yourself and others to prevent gossip, address issues and concerns directly and inspire speaking with good purpose.

> **Reina Trust Tip:**
> **Gossip and the rumor mill tend to run rampant during times of change. Yet, gossip destroys trust between individuals, within a team and throughout an organization. The consequences are devastating to relationships, morale and performance. In fact, our research shows that gossip in the #1 killer of trust in work teams.**

Trust of Capability®

This third and final dimension is all about having confidence in the skills and abilities of one another. You believe you're each capable of managing your responsibilities and performing in your roles. As you practice the behaviors that lead to high Trust of Capability, your confidence in yourself grows. And you gain awareness of your shortcomings. You become positioned as a resident expert, trusted subject-matter coach and a deeply competent professional.

The behaviors that contribute to Trust of Capability encourage people to be accountable to each other and enable the innovation that entrepreneurial teams and organizations need to be competitive.

Review the action points and questions below and gain awareness of how you can further build your Trust of Capability®.

Acknowledge Skills and Abilities of Others

- How do you encourage others to use their knowledge, skills, abilities and experience to achieve goals and meet responsibilities?

- Are you given the freedom you need to do your job, or do you sometimes feel micromanaged? If you feel held back, how do you respond?

- Consider where you could give employees more freedom to use their knowledge, skills and abilities to further engage, motivate and challenge them.

Empower People to Make Decisions

- What factors give you confidence in trusting another person's judgment? What factors do you consider when empowering someone to make decisions freely?

- When you've observed poor judgment in others, how do you respond?

- Tell people what you need to feel confident so that you can rely on their judgment and to provide greater flexibility and freedom. Doing so encourages a greater sense of ownership in their work and promotes their competence.

Involve Others and Seek Input

- Foster ownership in others and challenge their thinking. How do you seek their input? How do you empower them to make a contribution to key decisions or strategic initiatives and support courses of action?

- In what ways do you allow others to discuss, appropriately question, or challenge your thinking…and the thinking of others?

- Consider ways in which you can involve others more and seek their advice to gain their perspective and expertise in solving problems.

Help People Learn New Skills

- Uncover positive motivations in others. Are you able to rely on them to do their jobs? What do you need to see to feel confident in the ability of others?

- How are you creating a safe environment that fosters growth and builds expertise in your team or organization?

- Identify what support you need to develop the expertise of your employees and expand the capacity of your team or organization.

> *Reina Trust Tip:*
> *Helping people learn new skills is a powerful way to invest in them, enhance their confidence in their competence and to develop the capacity of your team and organization.*

<u>SUMMING UP…</u>

The Three Cs of Trust are mutually reinforcing and reciprocal. As you begin

practicing one set of behaviors, notice that the other sets also develop naturally. Additionally, you're rewarded as others in your organization begin to pick up on and pattern how you manage expectations, communicate and delegate. Trust creates more trust.

In addition, can support yourself further by using one of the Reina Trust Assessment reports, such as the Leadership Trust Assessment. The assessments will provide you with comprehensive feedback to improve the level of trust and trustworthiness in a leader, or among members of a team or organization.

Trust is at play in every relationship we have in life: both at work and at home. In all relationships, trust is built, broken and made vulnerable. Our trust is tested by the people we love, live with, and work with. And sometimes, our trust is tested by the very process of life itself.

You need trust in your workplace, on your team, and in your relationships. To get there, you must pause and consider your behavior and your approach to relationships.

Trust building begins with exercising the steps outlined in this chapter. It begins with you, and your awareness of the fragility of trust in your relationships. Do this now!

<u>Reina Dimensions of Trust: The Three Cs® Action Plan</u>

After having read and reflected on the material in this chapter, record the insights you've gained that have raised your awareness about trust building in your business and personal relationships.

Identify and describe all behavioral changes you're committed to making to support building trust.

Affirm the three steps you will take to make these changes happen.

1.

2.

3.

*For additional insight, find a detailed discussion of *Dimensions of Trust: The Three Cs®* in the books, **Trust & Betrayal in the Workplace, 3rd edition**, and **Rebuilding Trust in the Workplace** by Dennis Reina, PhD and Michelle Reina, PhD.

To contact Dr. Reina:

> Reina Trust Building®
> www.ReinaTrustBuilding.com
>
> Dr. Dennis Reina
> dsreina@reinatrustbuilding.com
>
> Dr. Michelle Reina
> mlreina@reinatrustbuilding.com

Jaxon Smith

As an intuitive, creative, and results-focused business leader with relevant transferable experiences in sales optimization and public speaking, my superior *customer service skills*, reception to *feedback*, proficiency in *public speaking*, and outstanding *mentoring* achievements give me the *confidence to lead others, build lasting relationships, and drive results.*

Provided workshops and coaching services for these clients:

Microsoft, American Airlines, Honda, Nu Skin, Assurant, Chipotle Mexican Grill, and more.

4.9/5.0 Satisfaction Score Average from 5000+ Coaching Engagements:

Organized 1:1 and group class sessions across wellness categories (e.g. health and fitness, work-life balance, etc.) to provide educational resources for clients using evidence-based behavior change strategies.

Facilitated 150+ Live Group Workshops with Diverse Topics:

Established wellness education materials and sessions for corporations experiencing burnout, stress, and in need of direction. Managed wellness presentations for various business groups and departments to build program awareness and drive user participation.

Largest Speaking Engagement with 850+ Attendees:

Delivered health and wellness solutions for corporate business employees. Providing employee wellness programming to boost productivity, employee morale, and enhance workplace culture for a Fortune 500 company.

The Truth About Habits

By Jaxon Smith

"It is the commitment to the method that will determine your success." Jaxon Smith

Bill Walsh made NFL history when he was hired at the head coach of the San Francisco 49ers back in 1979. After eight consecutive losses, Walsh changed the strategic method of his team—a change which led to three Super Bowl wins.

Coach Walsh had been hired to change the downward trajectory of the 49ers. What made his approach different was the meticulously successful system he implemented for his team. Walsh said, *"the orchestration of skills" and preparation*[1] is the difference between winning and losing. His method? He and his coaching staff began looking for any degree of improvement they could make.

- They observed the footwork of his passers and receivers to keep them synced with precise mechanics.

- Walsh created a sign for the team, stating, *"We will not be outhit anytime this season."* He had every player sign it as a psychological advantage.

- They practiced formations intensely until the offensive line could get the ball out to their receivers at unparalleled speed.

- When his players made mistakes, he intentionally turned his frustrations to the coaching staff instead, inciting a sense of guilt that led players to perform better.

- Plays were so rehearsed that if the communication in their headsets went out during a game, players could continue without direction.

The compounding effects of **continuous improvement,** in small degrees, led to a method of development for each player, which led to the progress of each play, which led to a championship-winning team.

"I directed our focus less to the prize of victory than to the process of improving—obsessing, perhaps, about the quality of our execution and the content of our thinking; that is, our actions and attitude. I knew if I did that, winning would take care of itself." –

Bill Walsh

Professional sports teams have similar ambitions. They all have an innate desire to win. However, every game—regardless of starting ambition or desire—will have a winner and a loser. A much-anticipated goal is not what ultimately determines the group's success; it is more so the planned and prepared method to achieve that success.

WHY IS THE METHOD SO IMPORTANT?

How does small-scale change lead to a winning team? How can you relate this to your own life? Those who have read *Atomic Habits* by James Clear[2] will be familiar with this concept. It is easy to overvalue the significance of setting a goal while undervaluing the impact of small-scale, daily improvements. The common misconception is that you need to set specific goals to achieve massive success. Whether getting your degree, writing a book, losing weight, winning an Olympic gold medal, or starting a business, you need to set a clear intention. This is right... to a degree.

We need our goals to narrow our effort on what we truly want. We need that focus to fuel our desire and motivation for forward-thinking and progress. However, we often put pressure on ourselves to make massive improvements. Meanwhile, improving little-by-little isn't always evident; it can be far more impactful and sustainable in the long run.

*The function of setting a **goal** is to have direction—to know the desired outcome.*

*The function of the **method** is to achieve that desired outcome— compounding effects of **continuous improvement** in small degrees.*

Day by day. Little by little. If you want better results in your life, career, relationships, and health, then don't focus on only primarily setting goals. It's best to take it a step further. A loser who sets the most incredible, thought-out, and inspiring goals without taking small and consistent action towards those goals is still a loser in the game of life. Focus on the planned and prepared method to reach your target.

BRICK-BY-BRICK

A lively boy, age twelve, and his younger brother, age nine, were asked by their father to rebuild a brick wall in front of his business. The two boys hesitantly said that the task was impossible. Their father replied, *"Don't you ever tell me there's something you can't do."* So, brick-by-brick, every day became a simple way of completing the task for the boys. Over the next year, the boys had finished completing this brick wall, and their father came up to them and said again, *"Don't you ever tell me you can't do something."*

In his later years, the young twelve-year-old boy said, *"You don't set out to build a wall. You don't say, 'I'm going to build the biggest, baddest, greatest wall that's ever been built.' You don't start there. You say, 'I'm going to lay this brick as perfectly as a brick can be laid. You do that every single day, and soon, you have a wall."* This boy is now the famous actor and movie star, Will Smith. Just like him, focus on the method. Take it step by step, day by day, and brick by brick. (Polluck 2014)[3]

MORE EXAMPLES

The McDonald brothers revolutionized the fast-food industry with their ***unique method***: the "Speedee Service System." This method applied the main principles of production and efficiency in their restaurant. They reduced costs by removing carhops and using a walk-up window, replacing traditional plates and silverware with disposable paper packaging, and minimizing their menu to only nine items to improve sales margins. The McDonald's Corporation is now worth over **150 billion dollars.** (Klein 2019)[4]

> "Our whole concept was based on speed, lower prices, and volume." Richard McDonald

Michael Phelps, decorated Olympian, is arguably the most excellent competitive swimmer in the world. His ***method*** while preparing for the Olympics: eating an average of 10,000 calories per day to sustain his strength and muscle. He did 2-3 workout sessions a day, swimming 80,000 meters a week (about 50 miles), exceptionally building his endurance. Knowing the importance of rest, he slept 8 hours with a 2-3 hour nap each day for growth and healing. This was his method for success. **Phelps holds the record of 28 Olympic Medals received.** He has more gold medals than 66 countries. (MySwimPro 2020)[5]

"Eat, sleep and swim. That's all I can do." Michael Phelps

In 1997, Netflix was created. Their method was to deliver DVDs to people's homes. Users could order movies on the Netflix website, then receive their DVDs in the mail. When finished, the media was simply mailed back. Despite the minor success of Netflix, in 2007, they changed their ***method of delivery*** to be more easily accessible. **It later became a streaming service with over 200 million paid subscribers. (Hosch 2021)[6]**

"Don't be afraid to change the model." Reed Hastings

THREE FUNDAMENTAL PRINCIPLES

Before we dive into the specific categories of life, and habits you can use for success, let's discuss three fundamental principles for creating your method for habit change.

1. MAKE IT SIMPLE

In simplifying a goal, remember that metrics are important. It's how we know when we have achieved the desired outcome. As an example, saying I want to lose weight is too vague and imprecise. If I lose one pound, I still lost weight. But, that one pound will not be life changing. Instead, ask, *"How will I know when I've reached my desired outcome? What would that look like? What needs to happen to make that a reality?"*

After contemplating these questions, imagine that achieving your desired weight equates to 50 pounds lost in one year. It's specific and measurable. However, many people stop planning there. They may start by signing up to go to the gym, try a different diet, or join a class. They start with ambition and consistency towards their goal.

After a few days or weeks of doing this, something happens—an event occurs, a distraction at work, or something to throw them off balance. They naturally turn back to previous habitual patterns and never lose the weight.

In your planning, you need to include a simplified version of your definitive goal: take that goal of losing 50 pounds in one year and break it down. That's 4 pounds per month, which is roughly 1 pound per week. Now that is something you can measure consistently! At the end of each week, you can track your progress. *"Did I lose the 1 pound yes, or no?"* If the answer is yes, you know you are on the right track and have the correct method. If the answer is no, you know you may need to change your approach.

Every individual's method and approach to lose 1 pound per week could be different. Like simplifying your goal, you'll also want the method to be in its simplest form. Perhaps it is to walk 30 minutes every day after work at 5:00pm. Or maybe it is to eat two cups of vegetables at dinner instead of bread and pasta. Or possibly implement intermittent fasting a certain number of hours each day. Whatever the method may be for you, make it a specific, measurable ritual.

Let's break it all down:

Original Goal: Lose weight

Measurable Goal: Lose 50lbs in one year

Simplified Goal: Lose 1lb per week.

The Method: A 30-minute walk each day at 5:00 pm

If at any point your method is no longer productive, you plateau, or are unable to continue with that specific method, change your approach. Discover another method that works for you. Then, track your results.

Instead of saying, "I am going to write a book in six months," say, "I will write one page every day."

Instead of saying, "I need to work on my marriage" say, "I will write five things I love about my spouse daily" and share this list with them.

Instead of saying, "I will lose 15 pounds" say, "I will exercise every day for ten minutes."

Simplify your goal and take it one step at a time. Track your progress. Adjust your method based upon a realistic timetable and your desired results.

"If you want a desired outcome, use a proven method that works."
Jaxon Smith

2. ASK THE RIGHT QUESTIONS

Often, when it comes to changing a habit, we naturally look for reasons to avoid. The mind is meant for survival—fight or flight. When weight loss is the goal and it comes time to go to the gym, the thought process is often something like: *"Do I want to go workout, yes or no?"* Most of the time, the answer is, no. *"Could I do something else instead of going to the gym?"* The answer is almost always, yes.

Perhaps the ambition is to make more money. When the time comes to put in extra effort at work to get that promotion, the thought process is something like: *"Do I really want to do that extra work right now, yes or no? Will it even guarantee me the promotion? Could I do something else? Is it really worth my time?"*

These are the wrong questions to ask yourself is change is the goal. These questions make you think of all the reasons you can't, or shouldn't, do something.

"The quality of your life is a direct reflection of the quality of the

questions you are asking yourself." Tony Robbins

Therefore, the motivation for change isn't achieved until a particular crisis, trauma, diagnosis, or event forces your hand. Essentially, you are waiting for some tragedy to initiate change in your life. When this uncomfortable and painful motivation comes, questions start to shift. *"What will happen if I don't change now? What is the pain or cost if I don't change?"*

Thoughts change not only how we feel, and our emotional response, but they also influence the direction of our motivation. If you direct your focus toward the cost of inaction, and the delight of taking action, you will begin to shift your motivation for change little-by-little.

Whatever you want to see happen in your life, ask these questions and be 100% honest with yourself. Make it as real and vivid as possible.

1. **What is the cost if I don't change?** Make a list. Make the cost of inaction as vivid as possible. *(e.g., If I keep eating junk food, I will be so overweight that I will develop diabetes, be unable to play with my kids, and could lose my spouse. I'll become depressed, inundated with hospital bills, lose my job because I'm physically exhausted all the time, thus making me unable to provide for my family, etc.)*

2. **What pleasure will I get for making these changes and acting now?** Make a list.

   (e.g., If I exercise 10 minutes a day, I will lose weight and have more energy. I will improve my productivity at work and possibly get a raise. I'll play games with my children, improve my relationship with them, have amazing adventures, and do more fun activities with my spouse, which will deepen our connection. I'll be happier and more confident in myself. When I'm more confident in myself, [fill in the blank])

"Remember, the motivation for change can be influenced and directed by the questions you ask yourself." Jaxon Smith

3. THE PATH OF LEAST RESISTANCE

When it comes to habit change, you need to set up your environment for success. Make it easier for yourself. For example, I wanted to work out every morning for 30 minutes to start my day. I set my alarm for a particular time and got started on my goal. There was a problem, though; my focus was on anything else I could do with that time. I could go back to sleep, eat breakfast, take a shower, or start my workday early. I did not want to take the time to find my gym clothes, my shoes, my headphones, my water bottle, etc. It was too much effort. I used these barriers as an excuse not to implement my daily habit. After contemplating this further, I thought I would naturally complete the desired routine if I eliminated all the barriers. So, that's exactly what I did.

I went to sleep in my gym clothes, so I wouldn't need to change when I woke up. I put my running shoes right next to the door, so I couldn't open the door without picking them up.

My alarm woke me up with workout music at maximum volume to get me pumped and motivated for a workout. I put my water bottle in the fridge every night before bed. Eliminating these barriers enabled me to follow the path of least resistance. I allowed my environment to support my habit change, versus taking me away from it.

Using smaller plates will naturally encourage you to eat less.

Trouble falling asleep? Move your TV out of your bedroom— remove the major source of distraction to make it easier to fall asleep.

Having your water bottle on your desk during the workday will make you drink more water throughout your day.

Want to stop watching as much TV? Throw away the remote; change the channel by getting up and using the buttons on the TV instead. After a while, you will not want to watch as much TV.

Want to floss every day? Put the floss on the bathroom counter and leave it in plain sight. It will always be there as a reminder.

Want to exercise when you get home from work, but instead find yourself sitting down to watch TV? Put your treadmill, stationary bike, or weights in the same room as your TV; do both at the same time.

Want to go to the gym in the morning? Pack your gym clothes the night before and put them near the front door.

Having a hard time focusing on your work? Eliminate any distractions on your desk and in the room.

Want to start saving money? Put a budget sheet on your fridge so you see it every day. Or pay in cash versus using a credit card.

"If you want to implement a new habit, put yourself in an environment that supports that change." Jaxon Smith

Research also shows that when it comes to making changes in our lives, accountability is one of the best ways to do so. The American Society of Training and Development (ASTD) studied accountability and found that you have a 65% chance of completing a goal if you commit to someone. And, if you have a specific accountability appointment with that person, you will increase your chance of success by up to 95%. (Hilde 2021)[7]

What would be the benefit of having regular accountability while pursuing your dreams?

What would the cost be of NOT having that accountability?

With my coaching business, I implement accountability consistently. If my client wants to lose weight, they text me their food journal every day. If someone is looking to improve their happiness, they message me ten things they are grateful for each day; we then follow up when we meet. I will provide techniques to create lasting change. We will set goals that align with our most important priorities.

Change your habits, and you will change your life—one step at a time.

If you would like accountability coaching, you can connect with me via LinkedIn –

***

To contact Jaxon:

https://www.linkedin.com/in/jaxonsmith/

References
1. Green Carmichael, Sarah. 2015. "How to Coach, According to 5 Great Sports Coaches." *Harvard Business Review*, February 25, 2015. https://hbr.org/2015/02/how-to-coach-according-to-5-great-sports-coaches.
2. Clear, James. 2018. *Atomic Habits: An Easy & Proven Way to Build Good Habits & Break Bad Ones* (Avery Publishing Group, 2018).
3. Pollock, Michael. 2014. "Inspiring Wisdom from Will Smith." *Michael D. Pollock*, June 19, 2014. https://www.michaeldpollock.com/inspiration-from-will-smith/
4. Klein, Christopher. 2021. "How McDonald's Beat Its Early Competition and Became an Icon of Fast Food." *History*, August 7, 2019, https://www.history.com/news/how-mcdonalds-became-fast-food-giant.
5. MySwimPro. 2020. "How Michael Phelps Became the Greatest Swimmer of All Time." *MySwimPro*, September 11, 2021,

https://myswimpro.com/blog/2020/09/11/how-michael-phelps-became-the-greatest-swimmer-of-all-time/

6. Hosch, William L. 2021. "Netflix: American Company." *Britannica*, November 10, 2021, https://www.britannica.com/topic/Netflix-Inc

7. Hilde. 2021. "How to Increase Your Chance of Weight Loss Success by up to 95%." *Get Active Online*, March 12, 2021, https://getactiveonline.com/how-to-increase-your-chance-of-weight-loss-success-by-up-to-95/

Laurie Cozart

Laurie is the founder and CEO of Brain Squared Solutions, an organization dedicated to using neuroscience to help create thriving organizational culture. She is an owner of Science2Wellbeing, an award-winning, evidence-based, advanced coaching program developed by high-profile scientists and coaches to increase life satisfaction through life-values alignment. Laurie is the founder of the Mind2Lead Institute of Professional Coaching, an organization that supports the ongoing development of coaches through coach training, mentoring, and supervision. Laurie is an International Coaching Federation, Master Certified Coach (MCC) a certified ICF Mentor Coach, and a certified Coach Supervisor. She has been featured in Smart Money and More magazines. Laurie says that being an executive and leadership coach gives her the extraordinary blessing of partnering with people in their reach toward their fullest potential. She shares, "I've had the honor of witnessing the transformational magic of aligning daily decisions with values, of fulfilling both life-long dreams and unexpected new goals. My clients continue to inspire me to do more and to be more." Laurie is the Program director and instructor of the UC Davis "Team Coaching for High-Value Results" program has been an Executive Coach and Leadership Development Instructor for UC Davis for over a decade and was the recipient of the UC Davis "Outstanding Service Award" for Inspiring a World of Learning.

Money and Your Legacy: What ripple effect will you create?

By Laurie Cozart

When you change your mind, you change everything.

The Ripple Effect

When I launched Brain Squared Solutions Inc., I had more in mind than providing for my family, earning a living at a job I love, or making a mark on the training and development world. My mission was to create a thousand ripple effects by serving individual leaders to become the best they can be. The leadership ripple effect impacts not just colleagues, teams, and organizations, but families, and ultimately, communities.

As the founder of Brian Squared Solutions Inc., I ensure our coaching, consulting, and training is based on neuroscience, the study of the structure and function of the nervous system and brain. Why neuroscience? Because it's the concrete side of psychology and emotional intelligence, and EQ is where the ripple effect has the greatest impact. As a leader develops more emotional intelligence, they increasingly see people through the lens of compassion and service instead of judgment and self-interest. They feel less frustration and stress and more appreciation and optimism.

Scientists now realize that our neurological systems send out tangible signals that influence the people around us. Research shows that kids whose parents come home at night angry because of work often become bullies at school. Our view is optimistic: When parents come home enriched by their work, they are more present and supportive of their kids, and those kids learn to build healthy relationships.

Money and the Ripple Effect

I believe that when you put your heart and soul into an endeavor when you learn your clients' needs when you develop the skills to serve, and when you honor your relationships and your commitments, the business thrives, and so do you.

More than forty years of serving and learning from clients have taught me that anyone willing to work at positive change can create their own ripple effect. In this discussion, I'll share some of my journey—delights, dead ends, and discoveries—along with some questions you can ask yourself to start your own journey.

Born in America

For over 245 years, America has been the premier land of freedom and opportunity. I was blessed to be born in this country and live at a time when opportunities for women would perhaps never be better. My parents weren't rich, but they managed with just one income to give us a nice middle-class upbringing. Both of my parents modeled a strong work ethic. In fact, I can remember my dad staying home from work only once—when he fell off the roof and broke both of his arms. Dad had a secure government job, but he also had an entrepreneurial spirit. He always had something going on the side to bring in extra money. For years he had a TV repair business in our garage. His 18-hour days followed a pattern. He would come home from his first job, take a nap, and then put in more hours at his own business at night. I was fascinated by the workings of the business, plus I really wanted to help my dad, so he let me handle some of the follow-ups. I enjoyed calling people and it made me proud to be part of my dad's business. When I got a little older, I learned that my dad's repair shop was his way to give back to the community we lived in. Often my dad would buy the parts and repair someone's TV free of charge because they couldn't afford it.

My mother was a full-time homemaker when my three siblings and I were young. When my older sister and brothers grew up and left home, Mom went to work. I loved to hear about her experiences at her job, especially, what everyone else said about her—how much fun she was to work with, how funny she was, how loving she was. People just adored her because she always made others feel seen, heard, and understood. As I'm writing this now, I am realizing how much my parents' approach to their work and their values of love and service has guided my own values and thinking.

My mom was very careful with money. I remember hearing "Money doesn't grow on trees," which often translated to "Whatever it is you want, we can't afford it." That, however, was the extent of their teachings about family finances. In those days, few parents talked about the family budget with children. The details of money management I had to learn on my own. In addition to their commitment to love and service, I learned three important principles from my parents:

- Becoming an adult means providing for yourself and earning the things you want.
- Work hard and take responsibility seriously.
- Serving people and building relationships is key to "success".

Learning to Work for Other People

I was elated when, at 14, I got my first job—waitressing at a family restaurant in Delle, Utah, a filling station on the I-80 corridor between Salt Lake City and Wendover, Nevada. Delle was 25 miles from my neighborhood in Grantsville, so I had to rely on an older friend for rides to work. After school and on weekends, I earned $1.25 an hour plus tips serving truckers, travelers, and friends. I had a blast learning about myself and others' worldviews and how important it was to keep your word and be responsible. Aside from the fact I always have and always will love to work, my job meant the beginning of independence. I had my own stash of money; I could go down to the local burger joint and play pinball or take the school bus up the canyon and go skiing with friends.

After high school, I went to work for a bank as a teller learning more about myself and the type of work that I enjoyed most, customer service.

I worked at the bank a year and a half and then transitioned to retail sales when a good friend offered me a cashier job at a local auto parts store. Cashiering was fun, I loved turning, what could often be stressful experiences into something easy and fun for customers just by allowing them to feel seen and heard. I learned a lot about myself and about maintaining resilience in the face of setbacks, and about how to important it was to keep a store running smoothly and customers happy. At age 20, I was promoted to store manager and took pride in a clean, well-run store, as well as in my ability to build strong, successful, and cohesive teams. I took pride in developing others and was known in the organization to lift others as I climbed, turning others into leaders, not followers. This theme of coaching and developing others has followed me through the rest of my career, wherever I went.

I worked at the auto parts store for 12 years while I raised my two daughters as a single mom. Even though sometimes I was buying gas by floating checks between paychecks, I knew I had what it takes to make it on my own. I had what I see as the cornerstones of my success, competence, and confidence.

Being a life-long learner, eventually, I outgrew the auto parts industry and wanted a new challenge, so I took a job selling property and life insurance. For the most part, selling property insurance was easy because people know they need to insure their homes, cars, jewelry, etc. Selling whole-life insurance was a different matter, however, because it starts with the potential client acknowledging the fact they are going to die.

Another barrier was that my sales efforts were mostly focused on young couples with families. I dreaded picking up the phone to cold call a prospect because I felt like I was spending my own money. I looked at my checkbook and related it to theirs. I remember one prospect's secretary telling me that I needed to "go to Helen Waite." It wasn't until they hung up on me that I realized the secretary had said "hell and wait." This adversarial type of interaction dampened my spirit and confidence. It wasn't until long after I had to admit defeat in this job, that I realized I had been feeding my own fears versus serving the client. Because of my own financial situation and fears, I didn't give them the opportunity to hear what I had to offer and make their own informed decisions.

What I learned along the way:

- I had the skills to succeed in many environments if I took the concept of love and service to my co-workers and customers seriously.
- Being part of a skilled, and highly trusting team is not only important to me but a key to my success.
- I loved learning and I loved continuously developing myself and others.

The Six-Figure Package

By early 2000, my older daughter was on her own, and my younger daughter was in high school. I discovered that I missed the excitement and teamwork of retail and made another major career shift, doing quite well in the retail fashion industry. I was a district manager for a West Coast company that specialized in trendy clothes and accessories for young women. When my regional manager left the company to start her own business, I stepped into her regional manager job. This is when I moved to California and brought two of my most trusted store managers with me to completely transform an area that had been underperforming from both a financial and talent development perspective. Within a year's time, we had transformed the store environment with beautifully merchandised and maintained stores. We had also successfully hired and developed a committed and highly-trained store staff who were on the fast track to promotion.

Our competitors watched as my teams created a 180-degree turnaround in-store performance, so I wasn't surprised when I got word that the director of stores for a big competitor was trying to recruit my managers. One of my managers introduced me to him, and we sat down one night. He said, "We've seen what you've been able to do for this company. Would you consider coming over to us as a regional manager?"

My first answer was "No, we have spent the last year working as a team to create something great. What would make us leave behind the successful teams we have created?"

The director said, "We will pay you anything you ask for and you can bring your team with you". This fell into my values of love and service; I could bring them with me, and we could repeat the ripple effect of success and grow and develop new leaders.

The ripple effect we created was felt companywide; our team approach to leadership and management allowed us to overhaul the corporate culture. Before we came on board the organization was struggling to transition from a family-owned and operated business to a healthy corporate structure. We spearheaded the creation of HR manuals, store policies and procedures, and the corporate operations manual. Our efforts turned the organization into a productive, structured, organized, and lucrative company. The changes we implemented increased sales by over 35% in the first year, increased the customer satisfaction survey results by 30%. Over the next 5 years, our team was able to open an additional 30 highly productive stores.

I had been working for the new company for about a year when the director was promoted to vice president, and I took over as director of stores. I negotiated a six-figure compensation package, including a 25-percent raise, which was written up in Smart Money Magazine. From the outside, it might have seemed that the deal was a victory for me, but in fact, we all won because I knew what the stores needed, and I knew what my team could do. I also knew this was a new opportunity for the team to step into bigger roles and further development. We all worked hard and took our responsibilities seriously, and we delivered time and time again. Not long afterward, the VP left, and I was able to step into his position. The focus on training and development, appreciation, and acknowledgment allowed us to create financial success for the organization and ourselves. But it also allowed us to create that ripple effect of more opportunities for others.

Jumping off

We were riding a wave of prestige and accomplishment, which brought freedom and power to execute ideas. It was exciting, and at times there was a lot of ego involved. Contrary to what my parents had told me, money did seem to grow on trees. Then I learned something about business success: Unless I was consciously and constantly consulting my set of guiding principles, I could be swept along on a covetous white-water rafting trip in a direction I didn't choose.

The company launched an aggressive initiative of building new stores. They broke ground and built so fast that they started to ignore the physical and emotional wellbeing of our staff. There was a lot of pressure to push people to do more than they were capable of, and the focus became solely on profits over people. My breaking point came when I was asked to lie and when I said no, they kept pushing. From that point, everything became tainted. Looking at it from their perspective, they might have said, "Well, we pay her a lot of money, so we should expect . . . ." But those were psychological agreements that I didn't agree to. They violated the long-standing agreements I made with my teams and my commitment to lift as I climb, not tear down to have monetary success.

Pushed too far, I got up in the middle of the night, sent an email, packed my bags, and flew home. I left with no job, no prospects, and no clue what I was going to do next. The experience taught me some critical lessons:

- I was vulnerable to acquired values that conflicted with my authentic self and must remain vigilant.
- I will always land on my feet. I can always figure it out – because I continue to value service and my relationships.
- I truly believe in the ripple effect and impact of leadership.

The Pursuit

One of the definitions of "going down the rabbit hole" is "to enter into a situation or begin a process or journey that is particularly strange, problematic, difficult, complex or chaotic."

That would describe my state then. So, what was I pursuing? For one thing, I was really tired of working for other people, and I wanted to use what I learned (both the skills and leadership lessons) from all those years in retail to help others. My former colleague had successfully transitioned from retail into coaching - I had actually been one of her first clients - so I decided to follow her example.

Why did I think coaching was for me? The answer lay in how the International Coaching Federation defines coaching and the coach-client relationship—a partnership aimed at supporting the client's goals. That concept appealed to me on a deep spiritual level – the service, the relationship building, and the inherent value each person holds within themselves. I could see the potential ripple effect, and I knew I could commit to a lifetime learning process as a coach.

Founding Brain Squared Solutions

The ripple effect we have created and the relationships we've built through Brain Squared Inc. have been incredible. We have clients and customers who have been with us since inception. The personal connection we feel toward our clients is beyond anything we thought was possible in a business relationship. We treat our clients like partners. We don't cookie-cutter anything. We customize all our offerings to suit their goals and needs. We do things for them that other vendors won't do, and we do it with a smile because we care about them and want them to feel seen and heard.

This partnering relationship is self-fulfilling. Our clients' growth and success fill us up both personally and financially and make us strive even more for positive interactions with everyone we touch. Each person takes from those interactions something of value, something positive that ripples into the lives of others. It's the legacy of love and service I want to leave for my children and grandchildren, the lessons I learned from my parents.

You can create your own legacy of love and service.

This is my story about love and service, and they have become my guiding principles in life and business. I want to thank my parents for showing me the value of service and building relationships, but I still had to learn by trial and error about what was really important to me and how to achieve my desired ripple effect.

Your journey and guiding principles might be different from mine. My hope is that you can use my story to jump-start your own journey of self-discovery and find out what truly inspires and motivates you.

By understanding what truly matters to you and what your guiding principles are, you can also take control of your direction, your interactions, the impact of your ripple effect on others – and ultimately your financial success. Here are just a few questions you can ask yourself to start your journey:

- What activities energize you?

- What values and behaviors are important to you even if no one sees you demonstrating them?

- When was the last time you felt overwhelmed with gratitude? Describe the specifics and why those feelings came up for you.

- If money were no object, how would you spend your time?

***

To contact Laurie:

EMAIL: lcozart@brainsquaredsolutions.com
LinkedIn: lauriecozart
WEB:

www.brainsquaredsolutions.com
www.mind2lead.com
www.science2wellbeing.com

linkedin.com/in/lauriecozart

Dr. Steven Greene

Dr. Greene is a lifelong educator and trainer. His parents were teachers, so he was raised with a strong passion for helping others and providing service within the community. He followed the 'family business' and earned a state teaching certification. He has held faculty positions at the middle school, high school, and university levels. In 1995, he established mAke the grAde, an educational consulting and training company. mAke the grAde has two divisions. The academic support division provides tutoring and academic consulting services for families and students. This enables mAke the grAde students to learn both essential academic information regarding their subject matter or areas of test preparation but also, he 'taught them to fish' by teaching his students life skills like time management and information management and how to establish a daily success strategy. These ideas crystalized with the publication of his best-selling book *Maximum Education* in 2015. mAke the grAde's entrepreneurs academy supports entrepreneurs and other businesspeople on their journey to success including workshops like the 'Five Structures of Success.' He continues to work with students all over the world virtually and through private coaching, workshops, and speaking engagements as well as live in his office based in Philadelphia, PA. Dr. Greene enjoys family, travel, cycling, vegetarian cooking, gardening, music, and being outdoors

The Five Structures of Success

By Dr. Steven Greene

Here is a basic truth: We want to get where we're going as quickly as possible. We live in a quick fix society. Think about your next vacation. Who wants to spend time in the car or on the plane? You want to get there and start having fun!

For many people, it's the same way in their business. You want to be successful and to get rich as quickly as you can. No one wants to stagnate in the same position for long periods of time! You want to advance yourself. And fast. However, I have repeatedly seen first-hand the frustrations people have regarding the quest for the 'secret sauce' to help them to attain their success. You feel like you are 'this close' but just can't get over the hump to the next level. You are frustrated because you're digging all over your desk for a note you wrote that's disappeared or you've missed meetings because you forget to put them on your calendar.

So, let's get right to it: This chapter is about accelerating your journey to success.

You're reading this because you want more sales and revenue. Your goals are straight-forward but they require consistent long-term focus and solid plan. As we all know, business success and the subsequent financial freedom and independence can be elusive and complicated to achieve without structure.

Everyone seems to understand this, so why doesn't everyone just do it?

They do not do it because they simply don't have a plan!

Here is your solution: The 5 Structures of Success.

The utilization of these structures every single day creates sustained success. And if you use them, you will find success as well.

Start by asking yourself some simple, but important, questions:

- How can I make my work environment the most effective so I can work efficiently?

- How do I make the best use of my time?

- Who will keep me on track, if and when I get off track?

- What are my professional standards?

- How will I get help when I need it?

Each of these questions will lead you to one of the five structures of success. The structures have worked for me, and thousands of students and clients I have shared them with, and they will work for you too.

If you are in a hurry, then here is the short version:

- There are five structures of success that work together synergistically.

- They are all equally critical to short- and long-term success.

- They require time and often some trial and error to set up, but once they are set up and in motion, they are powerful.

The five structures are:

- Physical

- Time

- Accountability

- Professional

- Support

Get these set up. Use them consistently. Achieve your desired results.

If you have a little more time, let's dig in, and let's discuss the role of each structure, how it fits into your life, how it creates your optimal structure, and how to use all of this information to create long term success.

Please meet your new friend, Steven Bizperson. Let's call him Steve for short.

Steve has a business, and he wants to be successful. But Steve is his own worst enemy.

When Steve tries to work, it takes him forever to get started because his workspace is a mess. It's his kitchen table or sometimes it's his picnic table on his deck. He likes to sleep in and sometimes starts to work at nine and sometimes at one since he is, after all, his own boss. Sometimes he feels like he gets a lot done in an hour and takes the rest of the day off. He used to be in a group with others who shared business ideas and networked, but he didn't think it was helping him and, besides, who wants everyone to know what he's doing all the time. Steve wanted to put together a set of professional standards for his business, but it didn't seem like his (not very long) list of clients was concerned about it, so he stopped doing it. Finally, Steve doesn't have people who he can call for help. A few weeks ago, his monitor broke and it took him two weeks to get a new one, effectively shutting his business down because Steve did not have a 'go to' tech support person.

So how do we help Steve?

Where do we start?

Simple. Steve must master the Five Structures of Success.

Let's help him.

Physical Structure

Steve gets to his desk (which also doubles as his kitchen table) about 11 a.m. on Monday and a mess awaits. He thinks back to Friday night, when he left his desk/table in a hurry because a friend called and asked him to meet up for drinks. He vaguely remembers being in the middle of a project at that point, but he figured it was time to start the weekend, and he'd worry about the work on Monday.

Of course, Steve's workspace is a mess. There are papers with sticky notes on them strewn all over the table. Not only that, but since he's used the space as a table all weekend, the papers have been pushed to the side in favor of plates and utensils, which also aren't cleaned up yet. Steve is out of sorts. He has a deadline for a client project at 4 p.m. today. He sets out to first clean up the dirty dishes, then make sense of the piles of papers in order to complete the work.

Steve needs to begin with the physical structure. He needs a well-defined and devoted workplace. If Steve were a CEO of a "real" company, this would likely be his dedicated office, but as an entrepreneur, outside salesperson, 'side gigger' or 'digital nomad,' Steve has to create his own 'success sphere.'

While this may seem simplistic, you'd be surprised by how many people lack these seemingly simple things in a productive physical space:

A desk or table, a comfortable chair, a functional computer and reliable internet, proper lighting, high level audio and video (especially in this age of video conferencing), and all the proper hardware and requisite software to complete his tasks successfully and consistently.

In short, this is Steve's physical structure, or his success environment.

It doesn't have to be complicated. But it does have to be 100% functional 100% of the time. Period.

With this in mind, Steve switched out his one large table for two smaller ones. He upgraded the lighting and invested in a good quality microphone. One table is now solely for eating his meals and personal stuff and the other one - his office - is set up with his computer, monitor, his tech, and direct access to everything he needs to be productive the maximum amount of the time. As a result, he is much more efficient, more focused, and he is making more sales. When he goes to his 'office,' now he is in work mode immediately. And now he has a consistent physical structure that promotes productivity and efficiency and sustainable success.

Time Structure

Steve tells me that he feels like he gets a lot done in a day and that he is, by any standard, productive. But is he really?

Remember on Monday, when Steve didn't start work until 11? Why was that?

Well, Steve set his alarm for 6:30 on Monday morning. He planned to get up, go to the gym, then come home and get showered in time to be at his desk by 8:30. But Steve was tired because he'd stayed up late with friends watching football the night before, so when the first alarm went off he snoozed it. After several more snoozes, he finally got up at about 8. He looked at his desk/table, and decided he wasn't quite ready to handle it yet, so he went to the gym. After his workout, he realized he didn't have any coffee to make at home, so he stopped at Dunkin' to buy a cup. By the time he got back and showered, it was after 10. He sat at his workspace and checked social media for about 45 minutes before finally getting around to working.

The first thing Steve did was to track his time for one week using a diary. The goal was simple: to see what he did and when he did it. Out of a 40-hour work week, Steve spent 67% of his 'work' time doing repetitive tasks like checking email and social media over and over. He spent 24% reviewing his websites and splash pages that were already complete and functional. He spent only 9% of his time really getting anything done: meetings with clients and prospects, writing proposals, delivering direct billable services, and interacting with other professionals to create potential collaborations and joint venture partnerships.

Steve did not "plan his work and work his plan."

This structure is improved simply by making a list of your to-do tasks, prioritizing them, then blocking out time to do them. It sounds simple. It should. Is it doable? Depends.

The 'Time Structure' system - to plan your work your plan - is a four-step process:

1. Make a list of all to-do items

2. Rank the list in terms of urgency

3. Block out time for each task with the most urgent first

4. Stay on task until it is done to completion

As simple as this may appear, the devil is always in the details and the quality of the work (more on that in Professional Structure). These are the 'core four' steps for time structure success.

Admittedly, this has been a difficult detail for Steve to master. What he's doing now is keeping a calendar on his computer, and constantly and diligently planning his time. He's color-coded all his tasks, with red being the most urgent. He plans out the amount of time it will take him to complete each task. And his favorite part? Deleting items off the calendar once he's completed them.

Accountability Structure

I asked Steve a simple question: "Who holds you accountable?" Sadly, he didn't have an answer.

And he asked, "Why is accountability so important anyway?"

Interesting question, isn't it? Why is accountability so important?

First of all, what does accountability mean to you?

Many people are scared of accountability, because it forces you to do something you may not want to do, or you only want to do it when you want to, not when you have to. You need to have accountability if you want to be successful.

There are two types of accountability:

1- <u>Self-accountability</u> is holding yourself accountable for what you need to do. Meetings, agendas, contracts, sales, marketing, hiring, returning calls and messages - all these are things you need to do to be successful in business. You may not like to do all of them or want to do all or any of them at a given time, but you have to. And you must hold yourself accountable for getting them done for the sake of your business success.

2 - <u>External accountability</u> is interacting with mentors/coaches, friends, a mastermind group, an online community who will hold you accountable for the things you need to do.

You're not doing this because you want someone to nag you, but because you want them to motivate you. You want them to keep you on track. Sometimes you need a kick in the butt to get things done on time. There is a power in committing to doing something. Once you tell someone you're going to do something, you have to do it. Find an external accountability partner you trust to keep you on track.

Every month, Steve has to make a presentation to one of his regular clients about the status of his work for the prior month. It doesn't take long. He gives a short update on each of the five or six projects he's working on for this company.

The problem is, Steve HATES making this presentation. He's not very good at keeping track of his time. He gets the work done each month, but he doesn't always write down what he's done or what date he's done it on. That leads to him frantically backtracking the night before the presentation each month, trying to figure out what he did so he can present to his client.

Steve needs self-accountability, and he's figured out a way to get it. What he's done is set an alarm on his phone at the end of every day. At six each night, he sets a reminder for himself to track his work for XYZ Company for that day. Further, he has joined a mastermind group where he shares goals with others in the group who keep him on track.

Accountability is challenging but critical to success.

Professional Structure

It is critical that you define excellence for your professional performance, and for the quality of the services that you deliver. Only you can control what you present to the world and to your circles of influence.

Think about it… you would demand excellence when you purchase a service from someone else, so you need to hold yourself to the same standard.

- How does the level of service that you provide compare to your competition?

- Is your level of service and the quality of your product superior? Inferior? Similar?

- How can you prove this to your clients and potential clients?

- What is your professional standard for yourself?

- What is your professional standard for your clients?

- What do your clients expect from you?

- How can you improve your professional structure?

Think about some things you've done as a customer, and then do those same things yourself as the seller. How often when you've been on the phone on a customer service call do you get asked to complete a survey asking about your experience after the call? What about when you buy something online? Have you ever received a survey about your purchase?

Try doing that yourself. Survey your customers after a sales experience with you. Don't make it long or arduous, just ask them a couple of questions about their experience. This is very valuable information. And then use their answers to improve your business.

For example, were your customers happy with how long it took for your deliverables to come through?

If not, address this by setting clear time frames in your policies. All work will be completed within 5 business days, for example.

Steve added a listing of his professional standards and what the customers should expect from his service to his website. He made a list of these standards that were reviewed, not just by other professionals in his field, but also by clients and others who had engaged his services. Now when a potential client visits his site, they have a clear and public declaration of his professional and personal standards for the business.

Support Structure

Some time ago, Steve was getting ready for a big presentation. He'd landed a meeting with a high-level buyer. He was excited. A week before the presentation, his computer started acting up. He ignored it. The day before the presentation, his system crashed. He did not have any relationship with an IT support team. He frantically called around for help, but everyone was booked, or they were only supporting existing clients on service contracts. Steve was desperate. He ended up going to a big box store and buying a new computer and spent most of the night configuring it. He did make it through the presentation. He didn't get the job, though.

Three days later, one of the companies he'd called to fix his computer did get back to him. They were able to get his system back up and running and fully online in 45 minutes for a cost that was $\frac{1}{5}$ of what he'd spent on a new computer.

The moral of the story is obvious: Have existing relationships with support professionals for everything that you do before you ever need help.

Think of everything you do in your business that if it failed you would not be able to function at 100% efficiency. Ask yourself this: what would I do or who would I call if that stopped working or needed support?

Here's the thing: you always need to know where you will get support BEFORE you need it. This is crucial for every level–no detail is too small. So think about it now. Do you have a computer technician you can call? What about a tax accountant? You don't want to wait until you're late with taxes. The last thing you need is to run afoul of the IRS.

Also, think about ongoing support. Remember the section on accountability? You should have that support person, coach, mentor, on hand whenever you need them.

How has Steve managed this problem? He's started purposeful networking. Not just joining meetings to see who happens to be there but joining with an agenda of who he would like to meet and what he wants to communicate to these connections. He made a list of all the essential services that he needs and is using networking to seek out professionals to help him with each of them. And the bonus? He has found that going to events, in person and on Zoom, has put him in contact with new people that can help his business grow! He's also been able to share his Professional Structure and core values with other professionals, creating a circle of high-quality mutual referrals. Win-win!

What's next?

There you go. You now have the five structures you need for success.

- Physical

- Time

- Accountability

- Professional

- Support

What will you do with them? How will you use them?

Keep in mind that everything is a process, and it may take some time to adjust, realign, and integrate the five structures into your daily habits. But it will absolutely be worth it to you. That much I can guarantee you.

So, ask yourself:

Are you like Steve? How do you be YOU and not be Steve? How will you establish your structures as soon as possible? What do you want and need to improve and how will you do this evaluation?

Contact me and let's do a complimentary evaluation of your structures. You can reach me by texting "INFO" to 2158253323 and, please, download my app - the Entrepreneurs Cafe - (on Apple and Google Play store) to learn more about The Five Structures Workshop, The Course Creation Workshop, and the Success Community as well as other collaborative opportunities. Thank you and good luck with your ventures.

***

To contact Dr. Greene

Text INFO to 2158253323
Email: sgreene@makethegrade.net
www.makethegrade.net
Facebook https://www.facebook.com/DrStevenGreene
Facebook business https://www.facebook.com/mtgrAde
Instagram @ makethegrade
Twitter @ makethegrade

Cornelia Dolmans

Cornelia Dolmans is the founder of The VIE Method™, and has founded and managed 3 companies herself. Born into a middle-class family, she was raised with the values of her father, who completed SOF training as a Marine, and a grandfather, who contributed to the resistance during World War II.

She worked for many years as a lawyer-mediator with clients around the world, from offices in two countries. When her career was booming and the future promised gold and brilliance, the love of her life was diagnosed with cancer that had already metastasized. The remaining time was unclear.

During a walk in the forest behind her home with ancient trees, it became crystal clear that everything in life has a price. You can't make an omelette without breaking a few eggs. The question remained what price she was willing to pay for what she had only just experienced: the perfect balance of life with a husband who adored her. Fairy tales exist, but they often last too short.

The day after, she began closing her law practice and turned into a 24/7 caregiver for her husband. After his death and a period of mourning, during which she managed to realign her Head, Heart and Hands, she rose again like a Phoenix.

As a business and personal development coach, she lifts her clients to unprecedented heights.

LIVE THE 5 A's!

By Cornelia Dolmans

"Visualize your Dream, Integrate the Alignment of Head, Heart and Hands, to Experience more Happiness, Abundance and Success in all areas of Life"

--- Cornelia Dolmans

The moment you are born, you land at a crossroads. From there, you can choose to go straight ahead or take one of the other roads that unfold as you look around you.

Each choice brings us one step closer, or just a little farther, from our ideal that we create in our brain as we grow up. That ideal image also can change over time. Many people think that it has to do with being lucky, or into which family you are born. Although that can certainly help from which point to start, the possibilities we have are unlimited. That is, if we make the choices and accept the consequences that allow us to achieve our goals.

Those life goals for you may be completely opposite of your neighbor's.' Where one's goal is to find the ideal relationship or start the ideal family, another may have a brilliant (military) career in mind or want to start or scale as an entrepreneur and be a millionaire within the year.

Oh, you want it all?

That's entirely possible provided you make the right choices, are a resilient bunny and reflect daily as you grow both personally, professionally, and adjust where needed. Each of us has limits, but those limits are many times further away than we often realize.

We can turn many more adversities into opportunities than we often think. We can achieve anything we want in life, as long as we are sincere, courageous, and decisive, have perseverance, endurance and stay resilient. Everything is directed by the neuroplasticity of our brains and the neurons swimming cozily among the dopamine clouds.

Did you know that everything starts with your brain? Yes, it does! And our brain also changes throughout our lives. The knowledge we gain through education, our experiences and our cultural heritage are all in the game.

Our brains grow and shrimp depending on our evolution from the day we're born into old age. But let me not bore you with dry knowledge on our brain and how our background and experiences affect its power, and thus our performance and its results.

If you are reading this chapter, you are still looking for a way to achieve or create your ideal life or to "bring in" the (financial) success you've been trying to work towards for so long. Then, for entrepreneurs and those who have or aspire to a brilliant (military) career, remember that if you ever fail, or have ever failed, that this is a gift. A gift, because it teaches you what is really important to you, what you could do better next time, and why you failed in achieving your goal. Every day, no matter the subject, no matter your age, you can make a new beginning. You matter, and you too can achieve what you wish! Step by step, or, with a little luck, in the blink of an eye!

I'm like weeds. Weeds don't perish they say. You can try to eradicate it, but it always springs up again, just like a resilient rabbit, who pulls his big ear from behind the big kale, after he has recovered from the hail that landed in his fur.

This last comparison evokes warm thoughts of the man, for whom I broke off my career years ago when I was almost at my peak. His nickname was "Rabbit." In writing this down, I am releasing a well-cherished secret of our family in front of a world audience. This makes me feel vulnerable, but aren't we all in one way or another?

After a marriage of 18.5 years, from which I gained three nuggets of gold in the form of three fantastic daughters, and the divorce thereafter, I swore I never would get married again. Wrong!

A few years later, the heavens seemed to break open when I met the love of my life. Both working in the legal field, having the same interest in history, travel, contributing to society and both raised with values like honesty, reliability and courage, the spark that ignited in that one moment brought Heaven on Earth. Our marriage was soon thereafter blessed by a Federal Judge in the largest state on the west coast with the grizzly bear in the flag, at the home of friends, supported by another wonderful friend, who arranged our reception in a school-backyard. Life couldn't get better. We had it all.

We travelled around, for both business and pleasure and took the best out of life. Nothing was able to overshadow our marriage, our happiness, and our future.

We had just bought a piece of land with a large area of forest behind the house. I finally began to believe that happiness, financial prosperity, and business success was assured for the rest of our lives. My dreams had come true. It was predestined. At least, that's what I thought. Wrong again!

A couple of years later he got his regular medical test, as prescribed for people working at the Court. When he received the results of his blood test, it seemed like the Yellowstone Supervolcano exploded. It soon became clear that we would have only a brief time left together. The cancer had metastasized, radiation therapy was no possibility due to the advanced dissemination for which surgery was out of the question as well. The specialists could not venture a verdict on how long we would have left together.

The question was how to go ahead. We realized how lucky we were, despite the current situation. We had everything our hearts wanted and had a good life with our three daughters and our two large Bernese Mountain dogs. We were also very well off financially and had already overcome so many obstacles in our lives, that we would get through this one too.

During a walk in the forest behind our home, I pulled the card and made the decision to choose my husband and the rest of the time we were given. Loyalty, making tough decisions while accepting the consequences, and leaving no one behind, are important values in the Military both under service and in private life. Both of us having grown up with these values and having lived them when we were doing well, meant that I had to live them in dark times too. For better and for worse, in health and in sickness ... just to name a few places we had promised each other. I had to choose. I did. The next day I started closing my offices and saying goodbye to my career as a lawyer-mediator. It was not easy, but it was the only right thing to do at that moment. Most people didn't understand, and we lost a lot of "friends" too. Clearing up friendships hurts. It's more alike after the divorce I went through years before. It also shows who fits in your Circle and who doesn't. Always looking at the bright side of life is not always easy, but it helps a lot, to overcome obstacles, painful experiences, and dishonest treatments by others.

We became aware of the real value of life, of what real wealth is and learned to be grateful for what we had conducted and learned, while being able to forgive those who hurt us.

Values that become important as the end approaches or when life shows you the hard way, when you almost hit the sky with your business or career. You all know examples in your own habitat for sure.

Now, several years later, having given these troubled times a place in my heart and still guided by his spirit, back on track, I want to help you get back on your feet as well, to get you achieve your goals, taking the next step towards your personal and business success.

After months of study and research I founded the VIE Method™. The Vision, Integration and Experience Method™. It is a never-ending eclipse that allows you to grow continuously to unprecedented heights, when implementing the 5 A's into your whole being.

Those 5 A's are also the foundation of my six-month course, coming with a nine-month group coaching schedule. Those nine-months, more often known by women as the time a pregnancy needs to get a healthy new-born on this Earth, is like a personal or business transition, when you really want to achieve success on the long-term.

Of course, there are exceptions, but most of us are not a hand-picked actor that instantly becomes a millionaire, because she's having that unique adorable look, the hero-character, and is able to manage her dragons at the same time, while being the star in the movie.

Keeping your feet on the ground, learning, exercise, staying focused on "the target," and showing commitment to the finish-line by doing what needs to be done, is the answer. It's taking the opportunities when they show-up aside, without procrastination, and working hard to do the job.

If it is a "Go," GO! But make sure to Do It Right!

How?

LIVE THE 5 A's!

THE FIRST A   AWARENESS

Self-awareness is a key step towards Becoming Aware of Yourself, To Be Your Own Natural Version, with which you've taken the first step to start drawing the blueprint of your destination.

WHO ARE YOU FROM AN OBJECTIVE PERSPECTIVE?

Sometimes it doesn't seem quite easy to answer this question, does it?

It includes knowledge of your desires, values, strengths, weaknesses, habits, traits, feelings, and more. It also depends on the values you're raised with, your cultural heritage and experiences you've carried along the way.

Developing your Self-Awareness by noticing your thoughts and feelings, learning to understand how you deal with frustration or emotional discomfort, examine your friendships, and intimate relationships, and keep a journal, wherein you also make a list of strengths and weaknesses.

A suggestion to start here with your own process is journaling. The answers to your questions may possibly change over time. Comparing current and past answers will help to follow your growth to becoming clear about You, and If or How your Ultimate, Best Life can be achieved.

THE SECOND A   AUTHENTICITY

Sometimes it doesn't seem quite easy to answer the question who you really are. It kind of depends on who you're around. When you're with strangers or co-workers, it's not uncommon to wear a mask or adopt a persona. You become part of the crowd simply because it's the easiest way to get along. Around someone you know well, this might be a vastly different story. The mask drops, the persona fades. You become more real, more authentic. You're quirky and a little odd, but a lot of fun. You're you. And that, my dear reader, is exactly what puts you ahead of the crowd, when you manage to do that in public.

THE MORE AUTHENTIC YOU DARE TO BE, THE MORE SUCCESS YOU'LL HAVE!

Yes, indeed. You are Good as You Are! It will empower you, as well as your entrepreneurial success, or as a speaker, a coach, a mediator, and every other way you present yourself, if you also got what it takes to do what is needed to do, to achieve your entrepreneurial goals.

A suggestion is, to start reflecting every day for 5-10 minutes, at the end of the day. Thinking of what you've experienced, how you behaved, and where you played a role, or have been more open, vulnerable, and authentic. Take that experience with you in the night and use what you've learned from it the next day, to become The Real You.

THE THIRD A   ALIGNMENT

When you're able to see and understand yourself clearly and objectively, you can say, you're becoming increasingly Self-Aware. Which is not a static thing. It evolves during your life, and it needs constant attention. You've also had the courage to stand out more realistic and Authentic to the crowd as the you-your-Self.

The neuroplastic of your brain got you to this point, making you Aware of Your True Self and telling you that you're worth being seen, that you can be successful without changes to be made on your authentic self.

From a holistic point of view, you could say your brain is the primary power-source. But you only can get out of it what it has to offer you, if you're involved with the passion inside You and taking the action necessary to achieve what it's offering you.

It's like using a broom handle to prop open a window. The window is broken and won't stay open. You know the broom handle will do the job. But is it pretty? Probably not. It looks like a kind of tacky. At the same time, the broom handle could easily be used for years.

When your brains are sending you messages what you should do, to achieve your ultimate goals in life, but your heartfelt passion is not connected, it'll be an extremely hard case to get the skills and achieve the success you have in mind. And when the action needed won't be taken because your hands are only holding a glass or the TV remote-control, you won't come any further also.

ALIGN YOUR HEAD WITH YOUR HEART AND HANDS TO INTEGRATE THE SKILLS YOU NEED

We start to think too much about *change* without realizing what we want is *transformation.* The two truly aren't the same thing at all. But often you need change, to get to realize a full transformation.

Only when you manage to have your brainwaves, connect to your heart-passion, and the actual hands-action, it'll bring you the power to achieve your goals.

Suggestion is, to add an exercise to your daily reflection, by listening to your brain, asking if your heart is in one-line with your ratio and mindset, consciously in the here and now. Take a moment to look back, to see which real action you have added to the alignment of the voice in your head, your heart, and your actions, and try to do better the next day.

THE FOURTH A   ADAPT TO CHANGE

"Intelligence is the ability to adapt to change"

--- Stephen Hawking

Dr Stephen Hawking is a brilliant English theoretical physicist with the same IQ as Einstein, like several sources on the internet say. Whether that is correct or not, fact is that his ALS, also often referred to as Lou Gehrig's disease, didn't keep him from working with space-time singularities, unlocking the theory of black holes, relativity, and quantum mechanics. Despite his disease he enjoyed a zero-gravity flight at Kennedy Space Centre Shuttle Landing Facility in Florida in 2007.

His body was changing, his disease got worse, but because he adapted to these changes, he could still do what he liked to do. And while keeping his brain busy, he became one of the most famous persons in the world who shows that even when your body doesn't serve you anymore as you would like it to be, you still can be successful in the field that you've pointed your goals to. This is a real example that shows that the neuroplasticity of our brains can influence what we can achieve in our lives.

ADAPT TO CHANGE TO GET THE SKILLS AND ACHIEVE THE WINS

It's the main secret of getting the skills and achieving the wins of every goal we have in life. It also underlines the fact, again, that you need to live the life that you want to achieve already in the now, to get it realized. That's why we need to align our aims with the way we approach live, work, and communicate, to adapt to changes, needed for a successful transformation on our way upwards.

In fact, you must integrate your wished-for environment and lifestyle as if you already have achieved your dreams. Sound more difficult than it is, but it takes full commitment, discipline, resilience, perseverance, and endurance to integrate it in your thinking and feelings and implement it as a natural ingredient of your actions.

Suggestion is to add to your daily 5–10-minute exercise at the end of the day, the question to the Real You, if you made any progress in changing the way you look at live, and already integrating parts of the wished-for-life in your habits, behaviors, and mindset. If the answer is "No," ask what is holding you back to do so and try again the next day to do better.

THE FIFTH A   ACTION

Changing your schedule for the next couple of weeks, changing your attitude forcing yourself not being you, or changing your thinking by visualizing yourself to the next level, is not enough. You will definitely have to change certain habits, adjust your daily rhythm to create your unique work-life balance, which will then enable you to achieve your goals and live the life you want.

Suggestion is, added to the evening reflection, to meditate for 5-10 minutes every morning to stimulate your self-awareness. Visualize what makes you happy and why. Think about your passions and ask yourself, what change you should make, to be able to live the life you envision.

Your action right now would be to **RENEW YOU IN 2022!**

Take that opportunity. Work Smart, Work Together! You don't have to do this alone. Stop procrastinating and let's do this!

To thank you for your time and attention you have put into reading this chapter, I offer you a 25% discount off the promotional price of my course.

Use **OFF25** at checkout.

Veterans get a bonus discount of 50% off the promotion price using coupon **SFUA** and proof of status.

START YOUR FUTURE TODAY AND CLAIM YOUR BONUS!

Let's make this world a better place.

A loose rein is good if you trust your horse, but you will first have to lead the horse in the right direction!

God Bless!

***

To Contact Cornelia:

Website   https://corneliadolmans.com

Social Media   LinkedIn

        https://linkedin.com/in/corneliadolmans

        Facebook

        https://facebook.com/CorneliaDolmans

Course   Platform   https://DMakeOver.Academy

        Email   help@dmakoveracademy.com

Michael Bolton

Mike has a passion for leadership both in the study of and its application in the real world. Traveling globally, Mike teaches, coaches and trains leaders in the for-profit business and nonprofit business settings. As a certified John Maxwell Executive Director and Coach, Mike utilizes the best proven & tested leadership material, to help individuals and businesses overcome challenges and grow in their impact & success. For over 25 years Mike served in the nonprofit sector as a teacher/trainer and also a college instructor.

Growing up in Canada, Mike excelled at sports and played hockey at an elite level winning a Canadian National Championship and an NCAA Division 1 Hockey scholarship. As a dad of three sons, Mike also trained in Taekwondo with his sons and earned a 4th degree Black belt as well as running a successful club raising up many other Black Belt leaders.

As a continual learner, Mike earned advanced doctoral degrees in both business and ministry and recently completed training as a certified Professional Board Director (Pro.Dir.). As a partner and investor in several successful companies, Mike brings his knowledge and skill to help navigate companies through the many challenges they face.

Mike is also happily married for almost 40 years, to a very successful entrepreneur. His wife Debbie serves as cofounder of Norwex globally and together they have three grown sons and five amazing grandchildren. They split their time between their homes in TX and Alberta, Canada.

Becoming a Great Leader - It Starts with Me!

By Michael Bolton

The most complicated person I have ever had to lead was myself. As a leader, we have to have a higher-level self-awareness than the people we are tasked with serving and leading. I heard the story of a leader who attended a training where he was encouraged to go back and share with his team his weaknesses and shortcomings. He refused and gave the passionate explanation that leaders should never show any weakness or admit any fault or shortcoming. His final question was, "if I share this information, what will the followers think of me?" The training facilitator gave a great response to the question. He said that the followers would have a greater level of respect for the leader because they were already aware of the leader's weaknesses and shortcoming, they just wanted to make sure the leader knew them as well.

The best way to lead well, is to be aware of our strengths and weaknesses. No leader has all the strengths and abilities to succeed alone, that's why they need a team of people who can succeed together. A great book that can help is "Strengths Finder 2.0" by Gallup with Tom Rath. This book has an online code to take the test and view the results. In life and leadership, we need to play to our strengths (80%) of our time & effort and delegate as much of the rest as we can (20%). When we delegate our weaknesses and play to our strengths, we will make room for others to grow, and the team will have greater success (impact and influence) in business and life.

In my current leadership role, I serve as a trainer and speaker to varied business audiences in multiple countries around the world. I also serve currently as a business owner and investor in multiple businesses in Canada and the USA. I have served in these roles for almost 10 years and prior to that I served in the non-profit sector and as a college teacher for 25 years. My additional leadership roles involve board management of the companies I own and continuing to teach and train on leadership principles.

As a leader we must be aware of the skills we posses and the ones we are lacking. There are three leadership skill areas listed by Lussier and Achua (2016, 2013, p. 9) and they are technical skill, interpersonal skill and decision-making skill. In my current role as a speaker and trainer I feel like I possess the foundational technical skills to continue to be successful. There are three areas in which I have gained a level of technical leadership skill. The first is through a combination of university educational courses. From 1984-1989, I studied in university and took numerous courses in communication, psychology, business and administration. I completed a Bachelor of Science degree in speech communication and had many opportunities during that time to serve in various volunteer roles as a student. Through case studies, research and multiple presentations, I discovered evidence-based research literature but did not discover the connection of the research material to the business world until latter. I also completed a Master of Arts degree in administration and through my final project, I tested and developed a model to train leaders in the on-campus group I lead. I also completed a second master's degree and further enhanced my skills in understanding various leadership models in the non-profit world. Over the course of seven years of formal training I learned the evidence-based research model but experienced its limitation for application in the business and non-profit world. In the years that followed I developed an additional set of skills in leading a non-profit organization. From 1989 – 1994 and again from 1998 to 2010, I had the opportunity to lead two growing organizations. The second one was over 200 people, and I was responsible for organizing over 65 volunteers and overseeing and managing a large staff. This provided weekly skill development as a leader. I developed teams and trained people to manage those team so in the end I only had to manage and lead 5 direct reports and felt more productive and less stressed as the organization continued to grow. I also had an opportunity to serve as a college instructor and college dean for four years, from 1994 to 1998. This was a new level of on-the-job skill development. As I reflect on the experience, the outcome was less than optimal, and I resigned at the end of the fourth year. I found myself trying to lead without the necessary skills and self-awareness and failed in the process. I spent a lot of time reflecting on that experience and learned the following lessons.

The first lesson I learned was that activity does not equal productivity. The Pareto Principle, or 80/20 principle, developed by

Italian economist Vilfredo Pareto, provided a model to understand business productivity. I discovered as John Maxwell states (2018, p. 34) that the top 20% priority activities I engage in will bring 80% of the desired outcomes. I have since changed the way I use my time and better prioritize activities I engage in. The second lesson I learned was to better manage my schedule and graciously say "No" to the many good opportunities that present themselves. Because I am more of a people pleaser and desire to get along with people, I would often say "yes" to completing a task that required too much of my time and could not get done in the requested time period. Even today, I would rate myself as average in the area of leadership technical skill.

The leadership skill area that I enjoy the most and have seen the most success in is interpersonal. The training I received came through a combination of multiple certification courses as a coach and trainer, and I accumulated over 120 hours of coach-specific training through ICF (International Coaching Federation). I am also certified with the John Maxwell Team as a coach and have additional training to the Executive Director level. Through this training, I developed a higher level of self-awareness and became more skilled at leading and managing myself and also leading other people. I have also completed basic and advanced level training in DISC profiling and analysis. This training has allowed me to analyze individuals in companies and provide positive and constructive feedback to help them get along with those they lead, their peers, and their superiors. I would rate myself above average in this skill area.

The third leadership skill level is decision making. For me, this area has had the steepest learning curve of the three areas. Through a series of successes and failures, I have developed good working skills in this area. While serving as a speaker and trainer and traveling extensively, I built a multi-millionaire dollar real estate business. I put procedures and processes in place and delegated responsibility to a small team to manage the business. Within a few years, I encountered numerous problems and did not see the real estate trends that signaled it was time to sell much of the portfolio. Combined with a lack of detailed financial analysis, the business suffered to the point of losing over $250,000 in just a few years. I finally liquidated all of the properties and learned some valuable lessons in the process. The most important one is financial reporting and analysis. I would now rate myself as average in this area.

As a business owner and investor, I now enjoy the opportunity to own a business but have very skilled managers running the business. I currently focus on governance and am involved in helping to set the vision and direction for the company. I also have the opportunity to work directly with the CEO and the operations manager regularly. I provide coaching and leadership development to see them grow and become better managers, primarily in developing their interpersonal skills. Currently, I only work with the top two managers in the organization. The material I currently use is from the book "Developing the Leader within You 2.0" by John C. Maxwell. In the book, Maxwell begins by describing the definition of leadership, which is influence (Maxwell, 2018, p.1). Many people believe that they should wait until they have a position to start developing as a leader. This may not be the best approach to developing as a leader. Tim Elmore, founder and president of Growing Leaders, states (2014, p.2) that even the most introverted person will influence 10,000 people in their lifetime. The question is, what type of influence will they bring to others during their lifetime? Another topic that I cover with the CEO and operations manager is the area of personal productivity. I work with them to help define the top 20% high-value tasks that bring an 80% return – The Pareto Principle. By using the model described by Steve Glaveski in his Harvard Business Review article (2018, December 11), we broke down the tasks that only they can work on and helped them to find ways to delegate the lower value tasks. By their own reporting, they felt more productive, and the company's financials reflected a change from losing money before I became a partner and owner to making a profit 18 months later.

There are two specific areas that I believe I can enhance my leadership skill in the organization. The first will involve the essential leadership skill of personal activity prioritization for all workers in the organization. A brief history of the company will provide a context for the value of this leadership skill development plan. The company operates in the oil and gas sector. Before my partner and I acquired the company, they had spent millions of dollars on R & D, developing cutting-edge technology that reduced costs and solved major problems for the Oil and Gas companies they served. The company was doing well financially and could afford the research with a plan to sell the technology and services at a future date for a very nice profit.

Unfortunately, the global oil market changed, and the company failed financially. One of the main reasons for failure was focusing on developing new technology but never getting to the place of selling the technology to their customers. The #1 priority for the company for the last 18 months is sales. The team of employees is slowly adjusting this priority in their time allocation and utilization. My goal is to help further the process and set up a simple yet effective system to help the team focus on the sales priority (80% of their time) and then allow for the R & D component and other duties to occupy the remaining 20% of their time.

The second priority involves the leadership skill of interpersonal connections – the focus on people. As a DISC certified consultant and analyst, this allows me to help the individual employee to better understand their own personality style and positively enhance their interaction with other team members. There are four distinct personality styles outlined in the DISC model. The first is "D" for dominant and decisive and makes up about 3% of the population. The second is "I" for interactive and makes up about 11% of the general population. The third is "S" for steady and stable and makes up about 69% of the general population. The forth is "C" for correct and compliant and makes up about 17% of the general population. When people recognize their unique individual personality approach (a sense of self-awareness) and recognize that others may operate differently than they do, there can be enhanced positive team interaction, growth, and productivity. My plan is to do a pre-training evaluation and then a post-training evaluation to see if any specific outcomes were affected by the training and skill enhancement. My goal is to grow the people, and they grow the business.

You may have found the information in this chapter interesting, but the real question involves your next step. In an era of constant change, we must be ready to grow and adapt. Here are some questions we can ask ourselves:

Am I open to change, and to what level is it demonstrated?

How developed is my skill in listening to others?

Do I ask enough questions?

Do I make too many assumptions?

Can I live with ambiguity & uncertainty?

Can I adapt quickly to change?

A great exercise is to rate yourself on a 1-10 scale in each area listed above. Then if you are brave, find someone you trust to give constructive feedback and let them rate you on the same scale. Now the moment of truth comes, how similar or different are the ratings? Now you have a growth plan, embrace the journey and grow in your influence and future success.

***

To contact Michael: www.LifeRekindled.com

References:

Elmore, Tim. (2014, February 20). Is Everyone a Leader? Psychology Today. (www.psychologytoday.com/ca/blog/artificial-maturity/201402/is-everyone-leader)

Glaveski, Steve. (2018, December 11). The Case for the 6 Hour Workday. Harvard Business Review. (www.hbr.org/2018/12/the-case-for-the-6-hour-workday).

Lussier, Robert N. and Achua, Christopher F. (2016, 2013). Leadership. Boston, MA: Cengage Learning.

Maxwell, John C. (2018). Developing the Leader Within You 2.0. New York, NY: HarperCollins Leadership.

Rath, T. (2007). StrengthsFinder 2.0. Gallup Press.

Eileen MacDonell

Eileen MacDonell is a fearless Intuitive Breakthrough & Performance Coach. She holds nothing back and loves to work with clients who are ready to play full out. Her mission is to inspire others to live unedited.

As a Robbins-Madanes Certified Coach, with a specialty in business, Eileen guides clients to the results they want. By identifying the blind spots that hold them back, they release what's not working, and move powerfully with a plan into who they truly are.

Daring to say what others won't, she spots what mental programs are running in the background, explores what's underneath and calls you forward to let it go. With her sharp intuition she knows when to push and when to hold space.

She takes her own growth and transformation very seriously, is always working with a coach herself, and is deeply humbled every time she gets to witness her clients' transformational journeys.

Eileen lives in Ontario, Canada with Super Husband Jeff and their three amazingly energetic kids. Thriving on good coffee and better chocolate, when she's not hanging out with them, coaching, or writing, she's reading a personal development book because the learning never ends… gratefully.

Stop Editing Who You Are to Serve the World

By Eileen MacDonell

"You better marry for money because you're not going to amount to anything."

~ My Mom

I'm the illegitimate child of a passionate love affair which explains a lot, but we'll talk more about that later…

For now, I want to share a story with you about how an unwanted and abused little girl became a soft, powerful, resilient, fiery, and fiercely loving woman who also happens to have a wildly successful life.

Growing up I knew I wasn't wanted because it wasn't kept a secret. My mother would tell me that she would try to take mustard baths while she was pregnant to get rid of me. A proven old wives' tale now, but back then she believed it.

When I was five years old, we lived in a triplex on a four-lane street, two lanes in each direction. Every weekend there were drag races and there was always this pink Corvette racing. I would stand on my tippy toes in my nightgown and, holding onto the railing of the balcony, watch the race hoping my Corvette would win. It was loud. I loved it.

That Christmas I unwrapped my very own Barbie Pink Corvette. It felt too good to play with. Holding it as though it was made of glass, Barbie would get in the front seat and ride around my bedroom. She won the race every time. Then, one day while playing out front on our driveway I noticed my brother and his friend down by the garage holding my Corvette. Only it wasn't mine anymore. It had been painted half red and half blue. I stood watching them with a trembling lip as I heard the plastic snapping. It was gone.

My brother called me a spoiled brat and told me how I always got what I wanted. His words programmed me to believe that getting what I wanted was a bad thing.

Children are great observers, but they're poor interpreters.

When I was nine, I had an ugly green bike with a red and white banana seat. I hated it but it was the only bike I had. For my tenth birthday I got the Blue Angel. Oh, this bike was beautiful. It was blue and purple, with a smooth white banana seat, streamers from the handlebars and of course, it had a bell. The moment I saw it I couldn't wait, I needed to ride it. So, as any little girl would, I jumped on my Blue Angel and rode her around the block. By this time, we were living in the country on a dirt road. I rounded the corner and went swooping down the gravelly hill, feeling the wind dancing through my hair. I felt free, I felt special. Getting back home after my ride I leaned her up against the garage and rushed in for cake. Within an hour, someone stole my Blue Angel. It was gone.

I always got what I wanted, then I lost it.

How do you think that worked itself into my subconscious programming?

Success equals loss. This was my story, what's yours?

Your greatest wound is your greatest gift to the world.

Our brains think in patterns. When one of our thoughts pop up, the rest follow until it closes the loop. The brain is always looking to finish the pattern. It's like an example I heard once, try singing Twinkle Twinkle Little Star without the rest of the verse. It's the same with our negative (or positive) thought pattern. So, when the negative pops up, interrupt it.

In a session with one of my clients she tapped into the knowing that there was something holding her back, but she didn't have a picture or words to attach to it for it to make sense. I asked her, what's your greatest gift? She replied, "ambition." Then intuitively I asked, what is your greatest wound? Diving further into that knowing feeling she described it as unworthiness. Her habit of ambition was born from the desire to stop feeling unworthy.

Whenever she was feeling unworthy, she tried harder to please, to achieve, to prove. So, as an adult, any time she would go for something she wanted, feelings of unworthiness surfaced. The pattern was programmed as a partnership between the two. It usually appeared as self-doubt and self-sabotage, and she couldn't understand how she could want something so badly yet end up at the same spot over and over again. Not getting what she wanted no matter how hard she worked for it.

By acknowledging the connection, you can break up the relationship between the gift and the wound.

You can't grow a banana from an apple seed and we never expect it either.

It's the same with our thoughts. We become what we think about.

What are the things you repeat to yourself, over and over again? "Why bother, it won't work anyway." "I can't." "They're already doing it so why should I?" "I'm too fat." "I'm too ugly." "I'll look stupid."

Going back to what I said before, children are great observers but not so good at interpreting. As children we hear what other people think of us, and sometimes we only have to hear it once and it sticks. In a fit of anger, in a sarcastic comment, maybe it's more frequent. This is called heterosuggestion: suggestion used by one person to influence another. As children we accept the words we hear by the people around us as truth and it becomes our inner voice.

Once we've accepted what others have said, what we've learned and chose to believe, the thoughts repeat, creating a superhighway to that way of thinking and therefore it becomes how we think most. Here's what we can do at any point in our lives: we can choose to turn the negative thoughts into a goat path and create a new positive narrative into a superhighway.

Creating that new route is done through interruption and repetition.

A practice I was taught by a coach of mine went like this; when you hear a thought come up that you don't want, say *"cancel cancel cancel."* Here's the thing though, you must replace the thought instantly with something you want in that moment. Let's say you're feeling uncertain, and this leads to a pattern of thoughts like "I don't know how to do this, maybe I shouldn't even bother, I've tried this before..." interrupt it. Replace it with "I trust my decisions," "I make good decisions and take action," or "I know exactly how to do this and if there is something I don't know, I'll find the person who can support me." Practice this as much as you can with any negative thought that comes up. You'll find that with repetition your goat path will become that highway to positive thought which will inspire positive feelings, which will lead to positive action, and then positive results, which will influence your thoughts, which will lead to more positive feelings… and so the cycle goes.

Like I said, we never expect to grow a banana from an apple seed so why do we continue to think negatively and expect to get the results we want? It makes no sense.

Positive feedback is silent.

It's common for people to require the validation of others. But what is most surprising is that we are asking people who have never achieved what we're going for. It's as ridiculous as asking that apple if it knows how to become a banana. Instead, surround yourself with people who have similar goals and people who have achieved the results you want. You're going to receive the right feedback at the right time from the right people.

Have you ever heard your GPS cheering for you when you're making the right turns? Does it throw you a parade when you've arrived? No. It notifies you that you've reached the destination and it ends the route guidance.

When we're on the superhighway of repeating thoughts, everything is smooth like fresh pavement, and then it's as though we suddenly remember we don't know where we're going. We slam on the brakes and come screeching to a stop. We need to ask for directions or ask someone if our driving is ok.

So, what about negative feedback? Have you ever heard your GPS scream at you because you took a wrong turn, and you should abandon the car on the side of the road because you're too much of an idiot to drive? No. It recalculates, gently. It demands that you make the necessary adjustments to get to your destination. Not stop. When you're getting feedback from the right people, that's what it will look like. It won't come in the form of discouragement and planting seeds of doubt.

Trusting your own GPS

Having accurate thoughts about yourself is critical to your awareness and your self-development. When you have a thought about yourself, practice self-observation instead of self-judgment. See the thought as just passing through and choose to watch it go by. Be interested in the thought, not invested in it. As it passes, ask yourself "Is this thought true? Is it accurate?"

When I had thoughts about my own business, the ones that told me that my voice didn't matter would show up most often. Comparison, self-doubt, planning without executing, caring what other people thought. "Who would want to hear me? Who would want to work with me? They're doing it so much better than I am so they're going to get all the clients…" The list of inaccurate thoughts was like that never ending train crossing when you're in a rush.

When you're hearing inaccurate thoughts, and you're not replacing them with something positive and accurate, you're accepting them as reality.

"I am the power I have been seeking." ~ You

I saw an episode of Oprah Winfrey's Lifeclass, with Joel Osteen and he was sharing The Power of I Am. He said *"everything that follows **I am** is going to come looking for you."*

That went deep. I finally got it. If I say I am something enough, then I really, actually, truly become that thing. If you call yourself stupid, then you think you must be stupid. "I am fat, I am broke, I am undesirable, I am______ ." Those are the results we get. We become what we say we are. We become what we consistently think about.

What would it look like if you chose words like "I am successful, I am powerful, I am loving, I am beautiful, I am worthy, I am consistent, I am confident, I am a magnet for money, I am ____________," and that's who you got to be? Notice how I said "chose." The negative narrative is the natural one. Ninety five percent of how we live, day to day, is habitual, it takes no thought. Want to know where your blind spots are? They're in that 95%. Most people go through their lives never hearing their own voices. Want to know what people think about? Listen to what they say, listen for their I ams.

So, what follows your I ams?

List them… Create your I Am statements.

____

____

____

____

____

____

To prompt me, a few years ago when I first started doing this, I had "I am…" written on pieces of paper and taped inside my kitchen cabinets. Then I had it tattooed on my arm. When life happens, I know I always have the choice of what follows "I am."

Having reminders everywhere keeps these exercises top of mind. They're my passwords, my alarms on my phone, the notes on my desk, they're on my mirrors in my house. Repeat them as many times as possible. Does it seem irrational to do this? Sure. It also seems irrational to not try it because it works.

Speak what you seek until you see what you said.

You get to become who you are destined to be. You get to claim everything that is already yours.

Always stretch into the brownie pan.

When I was little, I was hit and beaten by my mom until the age of 16. Being me, having feelings, expressing who I was, none of it was acceptable to her.

The definition that I carried of myself was one of lack, unlovable, abandoned. I didn't matter. Everything and everyone were far more worthy than I was. It was never safe to just be me, until I decided it was.

If you've ever made brownies, you know it's far different than baking a cake. It doesn't pour evenly into the cake pan. It's a thick mass that sits in the center of the square pan waiting for you to press the batter into the corners. While we're evolving on our own personal journeys, we get to stretch out into the brownie pan. We get to look at all of our messiness and be.

But first, you'll need to dig a little… who were you before the world told you who you had to be? That person is still there. The whispers you're hearing are from your play-full-out self. Lean in.

Who do you get to be, so you can do what you want and have everything you desire?

There is a truth buried deep inside of you and it's screaming "I just want to be me!" and you probably don't know what that looks like, not completely anyway. You've caught glimpses of who you could be and it feels strange and familiar. Would you trust me when I share that it's ok to take the step of owning all of who you are? That everything you want is inside of that knowing.

I remember the exact moment when I realized that all the greats like Napoleon Hill, Da Vinci, Beyoncé, Meryl Streep, all embraced their human experience. They stretched into their brownie pan. There I was this whole time trying to have a perfect experience instead of having a human one.

How often are you editing who you are so you're accepted, loved, liked, respected… How often do you show up as who you actually are, unfiltered…?

Be you, unapologetically.

Get your jersey dirty.

Find what lights you up, what sets your soul on fire. What are you doing when you do it for hours and it feels like minutes? And what are you doing when going without it for days feels like weeks?

Do more of that.

When I'm coaching, writing, studying my books, I come alive. Doing these things feeds me. They feed my soul.

One of my mentors told me, "Decide what you want in your life then say no to everything that isn't that." That's one of the best pieces of advice I ever got.

Go and serve. Give generously. Surprise and delight the people you find along the way. Don't worry about the "how" of how you're going to make money. When you serve generously the rewards will come.

The universe gives to a grateful heart.

Gratitude changed my trajectory. No kidding. I wouldn't have the life I have today without it. About 14 years ago I started the habit of being grateful. It not only impacted me, but it impacted my friends and clients and anyone else I've shared it with who actually do it.

When I started the practice, I didn't love myself at all. It was suggested to me to stand in the mirror, look into my own eyes and say, "I love you." Uhh, awkward. I think I would have rather done a snow angel on the floor of a grocery store.

It took a few years of doing it off and on until I didn't look away or feel strange when I said it and meant it. It was gratitude that got me there.

The exercise I did was this… I had a friend I emailed every day and shared six things I was grateful for and one of them had to be about me. Well, my hair was probably the first thing of mine that made the list, my eyes, my sense of humor. Then my laugh. Then, many months later, I found gratitude for cellulite, wrinkles, my bum not being where it used to be. It got really honest. I got really honest with who I am and how much I love her.

When you fall in love with you, everything gets to look different. It's like a light in a dark room that gradually gets lighter, and you don't even notice when it got so bright.

Love magnifies you.

Tony Robbins says, "If you want to blame them for all the sh*t, you better blame them for all the good too. If you're going to give them credit for everything that's f*cked up, then you have to give them credit for everything that's great."

I am so grateful to my mom who helped me become the fearless and incredible woman I am today.

From a place of love, forgiveness, and peace there is no more unworthiness and there are no more questions. There is a certainty of ownership of who you are. All of you, as you are, in this moment.

There is expansion and vulnerability. Play full out and love every bit of it.

I think she'd agree that it's a good thing I never married for money… I would have missed all of this…

***

To contact Eileen:

Email: eileen@eileenmacdonell.com

https://www.eileenmacdonell.com

Facebook: https://www.facebook.com/eileen.macdonell.1/
Linkedin: https://www.linkedin.com/in/eileenmacdonell/

Nicole Odom-Hardnett

I have never been afraid of a challenge or of failure," says Nicole Odom-Hardnett, CEO of Focus Point Solutions, which operates four Focus Point Behavioral Health clinics in Baltimore and surrounding towns. In fact, she always had big dreams, always knew she would be a leader, and always intended to be a business owner. But it was after attaining her master's degree and directing the operations of similar health organizations that she began to see how she might better her community and live the goal of being a "change agent." She works with a clientele that is struggling with substance-use disorders or mental health issues and the abusive relationships and other situations that often go hand-in-hand with them, while at the same time raising her voice to destigmatize addiction, anxiety, depression, and other diagnoses that are too often ignored or denied.

She's also done her own work and reflection. After a deep dive into therapy and personal development, she combined that knowledge and experience with her entrepreneurial energy and launched Talk to Nicole, a coaching consultancy dedicated to healthy relationships, particularly in blended families. She's part of one, a family that includes seven children and one grandson, and it wasn't smooth sailing at first, so she is quickly able to relate to clients who are also struggling to build connections.

Let It Find You!

By Nicole Odom-Hardnett

I am willing to bet that the reason you picked up this book is because you are eager to taste success and fulfillment in your life. Am I right? There is something lacking, or it is time for a change, and you are seeking a sense of direction. The question so many of us ask ourselves is, "How can I find my passion and purpose in life?" The answer…you can't. Now, hold on! Give me a chance to elaborate. You cannot find your purpose. Your purpose will find you. And once it does, you will ignite with passion and drive like you have never known before. Rest assured; you will be led right where you need to be. And it will probably be in a place you never saw coming. Regardless, it will come, and when it does, fulfillment will follow.

I have always been an independent woman. And I pride myself on lifting up other independent women. As a wife, mother, and thriving entrepreneur, I have learned a thing or two about success and what it takes to get there. It is my sincere hope that the guidance laid out in this chapter will equip you with practical strategies for meeting your goals and fulfilling your purpose. Straight truth, no chaser. You either want it, or you don't. You are ready to fight, or you are not. You will commit to whatever it takes, or you will allow doors of opportunity to close.

The process starts with taking a hard, honest look at yourself, your motives, and your desires. What do you want? Why do you want it? What are you willing to do to obtain it? Look back at your track record of past projects or business ventures. How many did you see through to the end? How many were abandoned before they even left the ground? What aspects of the venture brought you the greatest joy? What brought you the most frustration? Reflect on your life experience. Are there any recurring circumstances? Anything you have encountered repeatedly—anything that has allowed you to gain valuable personal or professional experience? Look at the people around you. Do they have experience, connections, and/or resources that support your experience or compliment your knowledge?

Your honest answers to these questions can make or break what happens moving forward—if you even move forward at all. They will help you hone in on your niche, your purpose, the little corner of life that God has called you to conquer. Your reflections will help you admit to yourself whether you possess the drive, the thirst, the force necessary to find success as an entrepreneur—because force is truly what it takes. Its not just luck or sound decision-making or diving into a hot market. Those things contribute, but without an unshakable drive to succeed, you will never get there. Success is found in what you know and where your skills already lie. When you really look, it will become clear. There is no need to reinvent the wheel.

So, now that you have reflected and concluded on the way forward, consider these five strategies to ensure your endeavor results in fulfillment and a prosperous outcome.

1. Do Not Take No for an Answer
2. Knowledge is Power
3. Do Your Due Diligence
4. It Takes a Village
5. A Growth Mindset

<u>Do Not Take No for an Answer</u>

The fact of the matter is, you will encounter a lot of nay-sayers— those who will be critical of your vision, processes, etc. Your true motivations for the future will never be clearer than when they are under the magnifying glass of outside opinion. Get clear about why you are doing this and hold onto that vision with everything you have. Do not allow nay-sayers to derail you, and do not change direction for the sake of anyone but yourself. People will always have opinions, but criticism without productive guidance and open-minded consideration has no place in your business plan.

<u>Knowledge is Power</u>

Learn everything you can about your new venture from those who have gone before you. Find out who is already successful in the field and discuss tricks of the trade with them. Seek advice from people you can trust to be honest and open with you about their journey to where they stand today. Be careful not to fall for anything that sounds too good to be true. Get-rich-quick schemes are not a reality for a true entrepreneur. Practice active listening to pick worthwhile strategies that can be molded to your advantage. Equip yourself with as much information about your new field/industry as possible before diving in.

Do Your Due Diligence

This point goes hand-in-hand with number two. As you are soaking in all this information from trusted sources, follow up with your own research. Check to make sure logistical processes and procedures are up to date. Confirm that what your sources have shared is accurate. Compare notes to see where you may have been given conflicting information. Do not take anything at face value. Do your due diligence, ask lots of questions, and confirm that the information at your fingertips will deliver what it promises.

It Takes a Village

Remember when I mentioned considering the people around you during your time of reflection? The reason that is important is because having a network of resources around you will determine how widely you can cast your safety net. Obviously, there is some level of risk involved no matter what the investment. However, the more connected you are to a dependable, diverse community, the greater your chances for success. These are folks who bring with them support and encouragement, expertise and recommendations, innovative ideas, and a variety of resources. Develop relationships with partners who are willing to mutually invest in one another— bringing an element of partnership that is advantageous to everyone involved. Build your inner circle of partners with those whose strengths compliment your weaknesses, and visa versa. This is critical. Networking is everything. Even now, I have been in business for almost 12 years, and I still rely on my village very much to keep my dream alive. If I had not utilized the valuable resources and people around me in the beginning, I would not have been able to establish the comprehensive team of clinical directors, counselors, therapists, and medical directors I have today

A Growth Mindset

If you do not take anything else away from this, please hear me on this point: you cannot let fear keep you from moving forward. You cannot be afraid of anything. You must embrace the obstacles and face the challenges, with every confidence that you will overcome. Acknowledge the problem, then shift your attention to finding a solution. You simply cannot allow yourself to dwell on the struggles you will face. A problem has never been solved by staring at it. You must act with intention and drive. Hang onto your vision, because it will be the only thing that feeds your motivation when the going gets tough. Be willing to do it right; do not cut any corners. Once you find the base of your knowledge and experience, set up camp and start building. Keep in mind, you need to prepare your mind for the long game. It takes a fierce work ethic. A growth mindset starts with the basics and allows room for expansion. Practice shifting your thoughts to constantly consider, "Where can I go from here? Where is improvement possible without losing sight of my original vision?"

When I was contemplating expanding my career, it was not immediately clear to me where my purpose was. I had personal experience in the behavioral health world because of a few individuals close to me who struggled with mental health and addiction. However, I did not realize this was my niche until I was presented with the idea to open a clinic. My husband and I were actually supposed to dive in together on this, but he came home one day and told me that he thought I should head this one up on my own. I went to the gym to ponder the suggestion, admittedly a little nervous about going solo on this undertaking. Sitting there, I was suddenly overcome with the realization that I was being asked to make a significant impact in the lives of countless people. I was being asked to care for them, to provide for them, and to step in as an advocate for their well-being. The realization, and the weight of the responsibility, brought me to tears. My heart swelled with anticipation, and I knew in that moment that this was exactly what I was meant to do. Giving up was not an option. People would be relying on me to see this through no matter what. Your purpose will find you, and it will represent good that is greater than yourself. It will set a goal that is more impactful than any goal you can set on your own. And it will be clear to you. You simply need to be aware and open to receive it when it comes.

It was not an easy journey by any means. Just because you are living your purpose does not necessarily mean the course will be without turbulence. After realizing my purpose, I connected myself with trusted sources of information, did my due diligence in researching everything I could about establishing a behavioral health clinic, and did not cut any corners as I worked through all the necessary processes and paperwork. Everything was coming along, just as planned. I had a location, I had staff, and I even had a waiting list of patients. The only piece missing was my Medicaid number. I had scheduled my inspection, which would declare my operation a viable business, but that is where my progress was stopped in its tracks. The inspector would not tell me when the inspection would take place. It could have been anywhere between two days and six weeks. Up until this point, I had been self-funded—fully floating the clinic on my own dime and a small line of credit for six months. I was paying for a brick-and-mortar and staff without any money coming in. I was not able to tell the patients on my waiting list how much longer it would be before I was able to serve them. I was heartbroken, discouraged, and frustrated. I cried a lot in those days. My moods were all over the place and it was difficult to stay motivated. I could not believe how close I had come to the finish line without actually being able to cross it. Forced to halt all forward motion, I waited with no tangible end in sight. I remember feeling so helpless; there was literally nothing left for me to do but wait and pray.

Three unbearable weeks passed before the inspection took place. I would be lying if I told you that walking away from the whole thing had not crossed my mind a time or two over the course of those three weeks. You too will face moments like this. This is where having a strong connection to the outcome is crucial. Cling to your vision and hold tight to the greater good of your goal. Pray, cry, focus, and fight! Entrepreneurship is not for the faint of heart. Do not take no for an answer. Do not shy away from the obstacles standing in your way. Only you can decide what kind of businessperson you want to be. Know your limits and know how far you are willing to go to succeed; do not settle for anything less. It is up to you to determine your future. Trust your instincts and have courage to step out in faith. This was the pep-talk I gave myself for three weeks. Perseverance saw me through. And today, Focus Point Solutions is celebrating almost twelve years in business. And Focus Point Behavioral Health boasts four, fully staffed clinics to serve those suffering with mental/behavioral health challenges. Harnessing a growth mindset, I have also expanded my services to reach a demographic that is very near and dear to my heart: blended families. I am the mother of 7 and my heart soars when I get the opportunity to love on and support other mothers who understand the unique joys and challenges of a blended family—especially when those challenges include the behavioral health and well-being of their cherished ones. My purpose found me, and it has carried me to greater heights than I could have hoped for.

I very much hope the same for you. Open your heart and mind to recognize where your knowledge and skills will allow you to do the most good in the world, and lock yourself into doing everything it takes to bring it to pass. You will encounter obstacles, you will be told you do not have what it takes, and you will experience moments of fear and uncertainty. You are the only one who can tell you you can't. You will absolutely encounter roadblocks but rerouting or changing direction is not the same as failure. Look at it as an opportunity for elevation and expansion. The journey may appear different from what you were expecting, but you will arrive at your destination, nonetheless.

Do you have questions? Need advice? Someone to bounce ideas off of? I would love to connect with you—especially if you are an independent woman, mother, or wife ready to take your career, relationship, or family to a new level. Women are blessed with a unique set of skills and characteristics that I would love to explore with you. It is all about community and support to embrace the fierceness of femininity.

***

To contact Nicole:

*Focus Point Solutions LLC dba Focus Point Behavioral Health https://focuspointbh.com/

*Talk To Nicole https://www.talktonicole.com/

*Savvy Sisters Society https://savvysissociety.com/

*Focus Point Home Care https://focuspointhomecare.com/

To connect with Nicole on her entrepreneurship and blended family expertise, you can visit her website or email nicole@talktonicole.com

Tony Vargas

Tony Vargas was raised with one older sister and one younger brother. At the age of 6, his parents decided to move from California to Veracruz, Mexico, to give their kids an opportunity to learn a new language and another culture. Leaving all of his friends and family behind was a difficult change, but he eventually got used to living in a new country; even though he was homesick, he decided to make the best out of this situation. He was very popular in school, joined soccer teams, and was always one of the teacher's favorites. However, at the age of 12, he fell and suffered from a brain hemorrhage. After surviving the surgeries, life was different. He struggled in school, emotionally and physically. Life became a challenge; he needed the support of tutors, physical therapists, counselors, medication, and doctors to achieve anything.

Having had a difficult childhood led him to desire to help others overcome challenges in their lives. Tony has a BA in Human Services, has been working with children and their families for ten years as a counselor, childcare worker, mentor, and Infant Developmental Specialist.

Tony is also an author, speaker, and life coach that focuses on overcoming obstacles.

Tony is able to give hope to families that have special needs children. He is a devoted student and believer in people's capabilities in overcoming any challenge.

Overcoming Victim Mentality to Succeed in Life

Tony Vargas

December 20, 1997, was the day that destroyed the dreams, health, self-esteem, and willingness to live for a 12-year-old boy. Yet, it was a day that started as a regular day. I went to school (my last day before Christmas break), played soccer with my friends, and enjoyed the Christmas party my 6th-grade teacher had prepared.

On December 22, 1997, I woke up lying in a hospital bed; my head felt like it was about to explode. I felt that my eyes were going to pop out of my head, my arms were tied to the bed, and my head was wrapped in a bandage. I had no idea what had happened. Playing at school that day, I fell and hit my head on the pavement. I started to feel dizzy and could not breathe, so my classmates told me to lay down on a bench. Before waking up in the hospital, the last thing I remember was closing my eyes.

After five weeks in the hospital, three surgeries, and a shunt placed on my head, the doctors allowed me to go home. However, they did not inform me that my life would never be the same. The first surgery the doctors performed was to drill a hole in my head so that they could get the blood and liquid out of my head, which was causing brain damage and would have killed me if they had waited any longer, but after they drained the liquid out of my head; I was still unconscious, so they decided to run some test to figure out one. I remember one of the tests because they put a camera up to my leg that traveled to my brain for them to find the reason for why I was unconscious. However, when they put the camera through my leg, I woke up and started screaming due to the pain; I also turned around and could see my brain on a screen then the doctor walked up to me and tried calming me down by talking to me, he then proceeded to give me more anesthesia and asked me to count up to ten. After that test, the doctors found the problem. They noticed that I had been born with a vein malformation; I had more veins in my brain than I should have, so that day at school when I fell and hit my head, it had caused one of the veins to rupture, then the blood from that vein rapture the next vein and so on, which led to the blood in my head. Once they had found the malformation, the next step was to remove the veins to make sure I did not have another brain hemorrhage in the future. This second surgery was extremely complicated It lasted eight hours and gave me the most prominent scar I have on my head. The reason was that they had to remove the skull to get to the veins. I remember waking up from that surgery and trying to feel the back of my head because the doctor had told my parents that my brain was so swollen it was sticking out of the skull; they also said that it was pushing against my eyes might cause blindness. I do remember not moving my eyes because it was excruciating. After that, the doctors gave my parents hope. They said that I would be okay and that they should feel at peace. My father left the hospital that morning to rest because he would spend all night with me. My mother would stay with me during the day, but the next day, when she arrived, the doctors said that I was again not responding and that I was not going to survive. They had sent me to intensive care, a place that I didn't particularly appreciate because visits were not allowed, and I felt lonely, scared, and hopeless. My Dad came back that night to find my mom in tears; he was confused because in the morning when he left, I was doing much better, and now once again, I was on my deathbed. My father says that he would whisper in my ear and say, "Tony can you hear me? If you can squeeze, my had once to say yes and twice to say no." He said that I squeezed his hand once; then he asked me if I wanted to live, and I pressed once again. The doctors once again ran the test and figured out that I still had blood in my head, and that was why I was not responding; they had to move fast because a brain under pressure would die. They then decided on a third surgery where they put a shunt in my head to drain the blood and fluid that was accumulating. I still have that shunt 24 years later, and it will be there for the rest of my life. My health improved after my third surgery, and I was eventually sent home. As a 12-year-old kid, I loved playing sports. I was very social and always maintained some of the best grades in my class. The moment the doctors informed me that I could never play soccer again was when part of me died. It shattered all my hopes, dreams, and desires. I was then informed that school was no longer an option because the hemorrhage I'd experienced had caused too much damage to my brain; it would be impossible for me to keep up.

The final blow was when my medical team informed me that the disabilities I was combating on the left side of my body would be permanent; my left hand was fragile, and I could not open it or hold onto things. I dragged my left leg a little, and my mouth was weak, which led to drooling—something a teenager did not want to be caught doing. If that wasn't enough, six months later, the doctors figured out that I was losing my hearing and would be completely deaf in just a few years.

That carefree 12-year-old boy, with so many dreams, went from being a happy, charismatic, intelligent, athletic boy to someone who was depressed, anxious, and fearful of life. My victim mentality started after the brain hemorrhage left me struggling with my health, social relationships, and a mindset that told me everything was impossible. For you, it might be an abusive relationship, a drug/alcohol dependency, a lousy childhood, getting fired from a job, dropping out of school, health problems, etc.

We all have a story; we've all had points in life when we feel hopeless. Overcoming the circumstance that left you shattered and piecing yourself together can feel impossible. These challenges often lead us to develop a victim mentality—a state of mind that encourages us to blame the event or the person that harmed us. We claim that everything negative in our lives is connected to that event or person and believe that we cannot move forward in our lives without dwelling on every wrong decision we have made due to that event/person.

Breaking the victim mentality is the key to moving forward with your life, accomplishing your dreams and goals, building self-esteem, having healthy relationships, and most importantly, living a happy and healthy life. The first thing you must acknowledge is that you played a part in all the wrong decisions that took place in the past. You must be willing to take responsibility.

You must accept that the person or circumstance is not to blame for everything wrong in your life; yes, we all face challenges. Challenges have no doubt held you back, at one time or another, and made your dreams and goals harder to achieve. Still, you must never forget that, even though attaining the life we want might be more complex, it is never impossible. The goal might take longer to complete, but by making small, consistent changes in your life, you will accomplish anything you set out to achieve.

Always remember that we have positive and negative will. You can choose to overcome circumstances (positive will) or to remain stagnant in the same life (negative will). The problem is, most people choose to use their negative will, and then end up stuck in the same habits, never accomplishing the desires they have for their lives. However, choosing to use your positive will opens the door to achieve anything and everything you could want. It is not easy, and it's okay to ask for help; luckily, we live in the age of information, which allows us to find what we need in seconds—at the touch of a finger.

Another thing you must never forget is that no one can control you; you are in control of your own person. It is not possible to control the people or situations around us, so learn not to allow your emotions to get the best of you. An excellent way to deal with your feelings is by practicing positive self-talk; talk to yourself, especially when things are not going the way you wish they would. For example, suppose you feel that accomplishing your goals takes too long and you feel like giving up on your dreams. Talk to yourself. Say something like, "[insert your name], I know things are not moving along as fast as you would like, but keep trying to achieve your goals, no matter how long they might take, instead of giving up before you find out what you can accomplish."

Another question you can ask yourself is, "What can I do or change to make things move faster?" You must be honest with yourself and pinpoint what you could be doing more or less of. For example, could you spend more time working on your goals by waking up earlier, spending less time on social media? Would you be able to accomplish your financial goals by creating a budget and cutting out unnecessary expenses? Self-talk has been proven to help rationalize our feelings so we won't make mistakes we'll might regret later. How many of you have made decisions when you were angry, frustrated, or sad, then later regretted making that choice because you acknowledge that you were not thinking clearly? Feeling that way is entirely normal, because when we make decisions based on our emotions, they are usually not the best option for us. So, asking yourself questions can help you make decisions based on maturity, knowledge, and common sense.

A victim mentality, depression, and hopelessness are typically linked to unhappiness or disappointment with the direction of our lives. Without a mission, there is no passion, no reason to wake up every morning. As a result, we feel unhappy with who we are, and we focus so much on the problem (or problems) that we forget to think about solutions. If you want to change your life and break free from the victim mentality, first change your focus. Then, explore the problem with only one objective: finding solutions to your challenge. For example, after the brain hemorrhage left me with a weak left side, I attended physical therapy for years. However, I reached the point where I was no longer seeing improvement. So, I made a list of things I could do by myself, like forcing my hand to hold onto things (I.e. a cup, paper, school books), joining a gym, and learning to use my hand to put on my pants, shirt, tie my shoes, etc. "What you practice in private will be rewarded in public," was my mantra.

Another thing I struggled with was school. It was hard to keep up with my classmates. So, I did the only thing I could think of doing; I started spending an hour or two every day with a tutor. Of course, there are things that we don't want to do. Regardless, if I had chosen to sit at home, blaming my circumstances and complaining about how unfair is, I would have never overcome my lousy mentality. Getting out of my comfort zone taught me to overcome every obstacle that stood before me. It gave me strength, vision, and self-esteem.

Once you have focused on finding solutions, set a goal. Your goal should include a realistic timeframe, what you expect to accomplish, and a reason for wanting to achieve that goal. It's essential to have a 'why' for changing your life, because you are more likely to stay consistent when you have a heartfelt reason. Setting a time goal is good because it helps you stay focused. But, don't feel like the time frame is set in stone; there are a variety of reasons why something might take longer than you want it to take, so make sure you visit your list a few times a month and make adjustments as needed.

Now that your goals have been set, make a plan. Your project should focus on achieving your goals. Start by setting your sights on small steps, and not huge ones, because big goals can be overwhelming. Not knowing where to start or where to go next is what leads most people to give up on their dreams. Zero in on small goals that will eventually lead up to your ultimate desire. For example, when I decided to start putting the buttons on my shirt/pants, tying my shoes, and just using my hand more for everyday needs, I began by doing hand exercises. Over time, my hand started to open more, and eventually, I began to have greater mobility in my fingers, which led to being able to button my clothes. If I had started trying to put my clothes on right from the getgo, I would have gotten frustrated, and would probably still be unable to use my hand today. So, make a plan that focuses on small goals that will build up to the big goal.

The next step is to stay focused. Human beings tend to give up when their focus is drowned out by the noise of those around them; what other people might say or think can easily distract you from your goal. For example, if you carry the attitude that your goals are impossible, or that you don't have the resources or time to achieve them, you may find people around you who will feed that doubt and enable further excuses. When this happens, make sure to look at your goals, remember why you started, and visualize what your life will be like once you accomplish your goals. Don't just visualize but try to use your emotions to feel how you will feel once you have achieved your dreams. Visualizing will help you return to a motivated state, renewing your focus on what you are working to achieve.

Once you have mastered maintaining your concentration and motivation, work hard on what you want to accomplish; make sure you schedule the small steps into your daily routine. We learn by trial and error, so don't give up if at first you feel that things are not working for you. Go over your plan, identify what you think is not working, and make changes as necessary. It's okay to change the method multiple times, but don't change the goal unless you feel you have outgrown your initial dream or have decided to dream more significantly. Don't allow trial and error to downgrade your original desire.

Take a lesson from history. As humans, we have evolved little by little, and every time we evolve, some things must change in ordered to make them work better. Imagine if the Wright brothers gave up the first time their design crashed. We would not have the fantastic planes that have made traveling great distances, not only convenient, but possible. Through repeated failure, the Wright brothers stayed focused on their vision and continued to make improvements until they got it right. Was it easy? No, and I'm sure they had moments when they thought, "Let's give up." Just as they identified the problem, changed it, and tried again, you too need to keep learning from your mistakes and changing your methods to find what works. Never lose your vision. The human spirit has been overcoming challenges since the beginning of time; make sure you use yours to accomplish everything you want in life and remember that action is the fundamental key to success. Hold tight to this strategy and watch your victim mentality vanish. Set a goal, make a plan, stay focused, and work until your vision is reality.

***

To contact Tony:
WWW.instagram.com/tonyvargas_thrive
WWW.linkedin.com/in/tony-a-vargas-84b55887

Eric Beschinski

 Eric Beschinski is an entrepreneur, business navigation consultant, speaker, and adjunct professor of business at Valparaiso University. As Chief Navigation Officer for Greenfire Innovations he is also a "B2B Missionary"; his higher purpose is helping others (especially small business and nonprofit leaders) find & fulfill their purpose then take their organizations to the next level.

The iNautilus™ methodology he developed over the last 14 years is designed to provide a visual, progressive, functional system of organizational navigation (strategy + execution). With 20+ years as a business-owner and over a decade in the financial services industry (credit card processing, banking, and insurance), Eric combines a strong mind for details/numbers with an eye for the big picture to bring a holistic perspective to business and personal development. His expertise in sales training and in B2B sales have given him a unique skill set and point of view.

Eric has written several books. His first was the iNautilus Guide for Organizational Navigation, and it details the iNautilus™ methodology for organizational leaders. The πNautilus Guide for Personal Navigation re-frames the iNautilus™ methodology for the individual (rather than organizations). In addition, he has been published on Thrive Global, Medium.com, Zapier Blog, and Entrepreneur.com. Eric has spoken on podcasts, radio shows, a Roku TV show, and national conferences.

Finally, Eric is a real estate investor, self-publisher, God-follower, and family man.

Saltwater

By Eric Beschinski

It has been a little over a year since I began a personal and professional voyage toward building a consulting business based on an idea from 14 years prior. In late 2020, I wrote and published the <u>iNautilus Guide for Organizational Navigation</u> shortly followed by the <u>πNautilus Guide for Personal Navigation</u>, and I started speaking at events to begin building my audience. Little did I know that my Ideal Destination (vision) would change as the original idea expanded and the intended audience shifted dramatically.

Part of this course correction came on May 21st, 2021. Right before my wife and I hit a deer on our motorcycle at 60 mph, I had a breakthrough in clarity surrounding my business, a breakthrough I had been seeking for months. That morning, myNautilus™ was born. That afternoon we were in the hospital. Even though we both could have (should have?) died that day, we had no lasting injuries and continue to ride. May 21st will forever be one of the most epic days of my life (you can read more about it at http://EpicDay.Greenfire.Live... It's quite a story.) The myNautilus™ is a holistic approach to life's core struggles such as work, interpersonal relationships, life purpose, and our relationship with God. Each of these will be addressed via a coaching/consulting program; it will take years and several other people to fully develop the material that myNautilus™ will cover.

An interesting phenomenon has become a pattern through all of this. I keep having new revelations based on ideas I had weeks or months ago. As I look for bigger-picture answers to various questions and problems, I "rediscover" a thought or idea and realize that it is exactly what I was seeking. That is what happened with myNautilus™, but it is also the pattern for the rest of this story.

As I was preparing a corporate training program for a client, I got further clarity around another gap I had noticed. At the center (literally and figuratively) of the myNautilus™ was a missing link, a core idea that touched and connected everything else. I had jotted down the words "water" and "conductor", but neither of those captured it fully. I frequently use a nautical theme in my programs simply because it works well as a metaphor. That is why I replace "journey" with "voyage", and I talk about an "Ideal Destination" rather than a "vision". Once again, I was wrestling with connecting ideas, and I realized that "the sea" is the answer.

Not only is the sea or ocean the medium through which a ship voyages, but it is central to everything about the ship and the voyage. Ships are designed to traverse the sea and withstand its many dangers, and the sea is what supports the ship. Life and death are in the sea.

The sea also has some relevant symbolism. In the Bible, the sea is often representative of "the people" or "the masses". Likewise, the water/conductor for which I was searching is all about the people with whom we interact throughout our life voyage. The ship represents the vessel on our voyage which might be an entrepreneur's business or an individual's life. A ship traverses the ocean just like we traverse a sea of people. Since God is sovereign over the sea, the people, and everything, I named the core idea, this water/conductor, God's Sea™.

I continued to find connections between God's Sea™ and the myNautilus™, but there even more under the surface. The sea is comprised of saltwater. Salt + Water. Taken individually, these two substances have almost nothing in common. They are seemingly unrelated. Water is usually a liquid compound of hydrogen and oxygen. It is a building block of life and often symbolizes renewal and transformation. Salt, on the other hand, is usually a solid form of a sodium and chlorine compound (both of which are toxic and dangerous when isolated). Salt is also necessary for life/health. However, when salt is highly concentrated it actually prevents life which is why it is used to preserve meats. Salt typically symbolizes purification and preservation.

Obviously, these substances are quite different, but when they are combined, something remarkable happens. The sea is teeming with life. Saltwater is necessary for life on this planet. It has a lower freezing point and higher density than water alone. In addition, saltwater is the key ingredient to electrolyte drinks which help replenish minerals needed by the body after physical activity. These electrolytes/minerals ionize bodily fluids. One of the reasons they are called "electrolytes" is that they promote conduction of electricity, and our nervous system operates on electricity. "Pure" or de-ionized water is an insulator; it does not conduct electricity. The ions that allow electricity to flow through water (and our bodies) come from minerals like salt. Oddly enough, salt is also an insulator. Yet when salt and water are combined, two insulators suddenly become an excellent conductor.

While that may be more than you have ever really wanted to think about saltwater, there is a point here. Combination of components often results in radical change. Even salt itself exemplifies this. Pure sodium, a metal, will react violently in water (as in burning & explosion), and chlorine gas is extremely poisonous (weaponized for use in WWI). When combined, however, we have a substance that sits on our kitchen counters, is safe to ingest, enhances flavor, and mixes safely with water.

Likewise, I discovered two seemingly unrelated concepts that when combined provide the key to navigating God's Sea™ on our individual voyages. These are Love and Questions.

Love makes sense. Like water is essential for life, love is essential in our dealings with other people. Unfortunately, in English we only have one word for "love" despite the many different manifestations of love. Ancient Greece can help some. In Greek, there are several types of love including eros (sexual passion), philia (deep friendship), ludus (playful love, affection), agape (unconditional/selfless love), pragma (long-term love), and philautia (self-love). In terms of our relationships, business and personal, the Greek words provide a much richer description than simply saying "love". I share that in part to help shift this topic from "touchy-feely" to a more intellectual discourse on love.

On my voyage, the topic of "love" keeps resurfacing. From influencers I began following, to book titles, sermons, podcasts, and even memes on social media, it has become obvious that this is a topic I cannot ignore. So, as I developed my mindset methodology, MindSetFree™, I realized that there was a piece missing. I had learned mindset methodologies from other coaches, and right in the middle of these there was a hole. This hole had something to do with love.

A moment of inspiration came to me at a local coffee shop as I was working on this problem. Right there, with my mocha on the table in front of me, I scribbled "logos" in my journal. The word "logos" is well-known in Christianity due to its rich spiritual connotation, literally meaning "word, discourse, or reason". More specifically, "logos" is the word used for "word" in John 1:1, "In the beginning was the Word, and the Word was with God, and the Word was God" (NIV). We also know this to be referring to Jesus, Son of God. Logos is synonymous with Jesus.

In addition to the innate spiritual context of "logos", in my program it is also an acronym. LoGOS™ means Love of God, Others, & Self. Phrasing here was intentional. "Love of" is bidirectional; it can mean both "love from" and "love for". LoGOS™ is all about love from God, love for God, love from Others, love for Others, and love of Self. The order is also important. God is first, then others, and finally self.

That order is scriptural. When asked what the greatest commandment in the Law was, "Jesus replied: '"Love the Lord your God with all your heart and with all your soul and with all your mind." This is the first and greatest commandment. And the second is like it: "Love your neighbor as yourself"'" (Matthew 22:37-30, NIV). In other words, make loving God your top priority. Then be sure to love others. And loving yourself is also a given. Simultaneously keep in mind that God loves you and others love you too; it's a 2-way street.

In addition, this principle is applicable beyond the scope of scripture. Think about what happens if the order is reversed. Consider Steven Covey's "Big Rocks First" principle. If you are unfamiliar, he has a story about a seminar speaker who demonstrates this principle by filling a large jar with big rocks and asks the attendees if it is full. When they respond, "yes", he pulls out a bag of pebbles and proceeds to fill in the spaces around the big rocks. When he asks if it is full now, the crowd is more hesitant. He pulls out a bag of sand, and fills the jar to the top, leaving no space. Except that, he then grabs a pitcher of water and slowly fills the remaining space in the jar with water. The point of the story is this: if you start with the water, you will have no room for the big rocks. So, put your big rocks (most important tasks) in first. Bringing this back to love, God is the "big rock". If we fill our lives with love of self, there is no room for love of others or love of God. If we fill our lives with love of others, we still crowd out love of God. Only by beginning with love of God do we also have "room" for love of others AND love of self. His love is all-encompassing and loving him first expands our capacity for love of others and self. We can actually love MORE by loving God first.

If we put love for God first and others second, then we absolutely should love ourselves too. After all, God does. We are his creations, his handiwork, his masterpiece. We are created in his "image". Add to that the fact that God sacrificed his son to restore relationship with us… All of this proves that despite our flaws and failures, we are worthy of love.

The second component of God's Sea™ is questions, specifically P3 Questions™ (purposeful, powerful, practical questions). Questions focus our attention, reframe our problems, get our minds thinking in different directions, and bring clarity & understanding to our relationships. A world without questions is a world without innovation, without connection, and the result is isolation and stagnation. Questions inspire movement. Purposeful, powerful, practical questions inspire *Movements*.

Science and innovation are founded on questions. "Why does that happen?" "How does that work?" "What would happen if we…?" Human interaction is founded on questions. "How are you?" "What do you think about that?" "What happened?" "What do you mean?" Academia is founded on questions. "What does the author mean?" "What's the solution?" Then there are the reporter's questions, "Who, What, Why, Where, When?" Our first response when we encounter something new is, "What!?", "What was that?", or "Huh?". All of that simply shows how foundational questions really are. But *good* questions can do so much more. Purposeful, powerful, practical questions can potentially change the world.

To implement and utilize P3 Questions™ effectively, it helps to know how to form them. These are not rules; they are just guidelines to help ensure your questions are purposeful, powerful, and practical. First an example: rather than ask, "How can we improve the automobile seatbelt?", ask "What can we add to the automobile seatbelt that will dramatically improve safety AND comfort for the wearer?" It may also help to look at each of the three p-words separately.

A **purpose** is the "why". Although sometimes the "why" is implied in a question, when it comes to everyday situations, clearly stating the "why" in the question can be extremely valuable. In the seatbelt example, the phrase, "…that will dramatically improve safety AND comfort for the wearer," effectively addresses the "why" component and gives the question purpose.

There are many ways to make a question **powerful**. Specificity can help transform an ordinary question to a P3 Question™. More specific questions help engage the creative engine in your mind. We tend to think that greater possibility allows our minds to be freer and more innovative, but the opposite is true. Wide-open, empty space can be difficult to fill. Without prior inspiration (something that sparked an idea), trying to paint on a blank canvas or write on a blank screen is often daunting. However, when given parameters, limitations, or *boundaries*, our minds are free to focus and generate ideas. Simply using the word "add" instead of "improve" in the example makes the question more specific. That in turn adds power to the question.

Practicality is all about movement. A P3 Question™ should propel us forward. Especially in business, ensuring our questions are practical will contribute to the energy surrounding them. They should involve real problems or anticipated situations. They should lead to better products/services, higher profitability, or simply solutions. Addressing the safety and comfort of drivers and passengers in our example is very practical.

With a better understanding of P3 Questions™, now you might be wondering how questions relate back to love. When you combine love and questions, you get a new body of "saltwater". God's Sea™ becomes a medium where our motives and motion are aligned. Love is the antithesis to fear. Questions are the antithesis to apathy. Fear and apathy are two of the most significant and damaging blights on our 21st century culture. Love + Questions—amidst the people we encounter on our voyage—creates hope, and hope is what enables humanity to thrive.

Practically speaking though, how do we live this out? In business, we need to put God first. We are stewards of everything he has given us (which encompasses everything we have). None of it really belongs to us. So, we need to ask things like:

> "What would the Owner (God) want me to do with this business?"

> "How could I honor God with this decision?"

We also need to remember that God loves us, so P3 Questions™ might be:

> "With what has God blessed me that I can enjoy right now?"

> "What are the opportunities behind this challenge?"

As for loving other people, consider asking yourself:

> "How can I employ my business to help others (in a more meaningful way)?"

When you see someone struggling, instead of asking how you can help, try offering something specific.

> "I saw you were struggling with _________. Would it be helpful if I _________?"

From the perspective of people who are loved by other people, pose questions such as:

> "Did they mean to be hurtful, or am I creating a false story about that experience?"

> "Would this action make [loved one] proud of me or disappointed in me?"

Finally, we need to look inward.

> "I am a Child of God. Is this (action/course/decision) what a Child of God would do?"

> "What action can I take today to become more like the person God designed me to be?"

Of course, these are only a few examples. The list of possible P3 Questions™ you can ask yourself and others (and God) is virtually limitless. Use questions like these to align your motives and motion so that you can have a purposeful, powerful, practical, and loving impact on the world.

***

To contact Eric:

Website: www.GreenfireInnovations.com/hello

Email: Eric@GreenfireInnovations.com

LinkedIn: LinkedIn.Beschinski.com

Jonathan Glass ND, M.Ac.

Jonathan Glass ND, M.Ac. is a Naturopathc Doctor, Master Acupuncturist, Ayurvedic Practitioner, Energy Healer, Hypnotherapist and Natural Health Educator. He is the author and founder of *The Total Life Cleanse: A 28 Day Program to Detoxify and Nourish Body, Mind and Soul*. Jonathan served on the faculty of The Dharma Institute of Yoga and Ayurveda and the New England School of Acupuncture. He has facilitated thousands through his group and individually based Total Life Cleanse program.

Jonathan studied massage therapy, hypnotherapy and nutrition at Heartwood Institute in California and acupuncture at the Worsley Institute for Classical Acupuncture in Florida and the College of Traditional Acupuncture in England. He received his Masters in acupuncture at the Academy of Five Element Acupuncture in Florida. Jonathan received his naturopathic doctor's degree from the University of Natural Medicine. In his busy private practice, Jonathan utilizes acupuncture, dietary/lifestyle recommendations, herbs, nutrients and various forms of Muscle Response Testing such as Nutrition Response Testing and Health Scan Technique. He has also trained extensively in Ayurveda, yoga, and meditation while living in India, and through the American Institute of Vedic Studies and the Dharma Institute of Yoga and Ayurveda. Integrating his years of experience with the many tools and modalities he practices, Jonathan works intensively and individually with each student and patient. In 1992 Jonathan Co-founded the Healing Essence Center in, a multi practitioner healing center in West Concord, Massachusetts, with his wife Katherine.

Living Your Purpose Through High Level Health

By Jonathan Glass

As a health practitioner and entrepreneur, I have realized the value of experiencing high level energy and health in body and mind. Years ago, I discovered the essential principles of health that transformed my life. Sharing them became my calling, especially after overcoming my own health challenges in my twenties. The following draws from my knowledge of ancient-health wisdom, modern nutritional science and years of working with thousands of patients, many of them entrepreneurs. I've experienced firsthand the significance of vitality and good health when it comes to running a business and maintaining positive relationships.

Entrepreneurs must consistently maintain high energy levels and mental focus, in order to achieve success. Typically, they are creative and energetic people! Sometimes, passion for success distracts them from their diligence regarding health and wellbeing. It's generally not an issue through their thirties however in time, reactions to sub-optimal dietary and lifestyle habits tend to manifest. Symptoms often begin with fatigue and evolve to weight gain, pain, and mental fog. If ignored, cardiovascular, blood-sugar and immune related issues can occur. Some who are quite successful retire early to enjoy comfortable lives. Sadly, many find that their tension-free days turn into stress filled nights due to nagging health challenges. That's why it's essential to implement effective health practices!

I hope the following inspires you to nurture your wellbeing and attain fulfillment in all the ways that really matter.

Foundational Health Pillars: Diet, Lifestyle and Cleansing

I've found the most effective way to avoid health related pitfalls is to reclaim our energy and wellbeing through optimal dietary, lifestyle and detoxification practices. Cleansing is the process of making dietary, herbal, and lifestyle choices that encourage safe detoxification and rejuvenation in body and mind.

Such practices have been recommended for thousands of years. Detoxification or cleansing benefits are not so well known, but they're more relevant now than ever!

For years there's been a disregard for the impact toxins, drugs, diet and lifestyle have on our well-being. Fortunately, there's recently been a greater appreciation for clean eating, exercise, yoga, ayurveda (the science of life), acupuncture, and detoxification (cleansing).

Many approach a clean diet and cleansing to lose weight and feel better. Some hope to strengthen immunity, manage disease, lower blood pressure, decrease pain, and improve digestion and sleep. Others employ cleansing to reset and reconnect to better habits.

Eliminating stored toxins balances the nervous system, improves our nutritional status and enhances our immunity, vitality, and mental and spiritual clarity. It helps us feel energized, enthusiastic, and really good again!

What Is Cleansing?

Cleansing is the process of making health-enhancing and detoxifying dietary and lifestyle changes that enhance our natural well-being. It is a focused method of relieving the body and mind from the burden of toxicity and harmful stress. Bi-yearly cleansing offers the greatest benefits. It's remarkable how positively the body and mind rebalance when given the opportunity. Cleansing with a mindful approach is best to avoid unnecessary detox reactions, otherwise, benefits gained can be lost.

The ancient wisdom of Chinese medicine follows the principle "fu zheng qu xie", which means "'dispel evil by supporting the righteous." This means in order to fight disease we must expel toxins and destroy infectious pathogens while simultaneously strengthening our immune system with a clean, nutritious diet and healthy lifestyle.

Why Cleanse? Stressed, Starved and Poisoned

We are living in challenging times due to constant stress, poor nutrition and environmental toxins. We are stressed, starved and poisoned. Unless we're proactive, these challenges nibble away at our energy, productivity, creativity, health, and sanity! Never before have we been exposed to such a barrage of toxins, including biological (viruses, bacteria, parasitic, fungal), dietary, chemical, heavy metal, and radioactive, as well as modern-day emotional and spiritual stressors.

The nutritional quality of our food has also significantly diminished in the past fifty years. The synergistic effect of stress, nutritional depletion and toxicity, can have a devastating impact on our overall well-being.

The good news is that these challenges can be significantly reduced or even eliminated through favorable dietary, lifestyle and cleansing practices.

A successful cleanse:
· Reduces pain
· Improves digestion
· Enhances energy, focus, mood and productivity
· Strengthens immunity
· Reduces cravings for junk food
· Increases attraction to whole foods
· Stimulates weight loss
· Empowers confidence
· Heightens awareness of one's life purpose

These are just some of the rewards that come when we take our health and lives into our own hands through clean eating and cleansing! The broad intention of cleansing is to increase awareness of the interconnectedness of life, and to realize our full potential as human beings.

Essential Principles of Health

The following essential principles of health are based on the ancient wisdom of ayurveda, which is the "the science of life". These principles give a clear understanding of the original cause of health and disease as well as the extraordinary value of cleansing. Anyone interested in personal development and success can benefit by appreciating this profound wisdom.

Originating in ancient India, ayurveda is the original contributor to the practices of natural health and healing on this planet. For example, most natural systems of healing, including herbology, massage therapy, chiropractic, and even acupuncture draw from ayurveda. While dating back thousands of years, ayurveda is scientific, highly effective, and full of commonsense. Don't be intimidated by the exotic sounding Sanskrit words below, as you'll find their essential meaning to be practical, thought provoking and enlightening.

The Essential Principles of Ayurveda:
Prajnaparadha: original cause of disease
Ama: toxins
Buddhi: innate intelligence
Prana: vital life-energy
Agni: fire of digestion
Ojas: essence of immunity
Details on the Principles:
Prajnaparadha (prag-yapa-rada): The Cause of All Disease

Prajna (pragya) means knowledge which includes our experience, intuition, and wisdom. *Aparadha* means to ignore or offend. *Prajnaparadha* is the act of offending, ignoring, or denying our innate wisdom, intuition, and knowledge gained through experience. It's our inner gremlin or saboteur and is known as the primary cause of disease.

Prajnaparadha results in actions that knowingly cause distress. It arises quite innocently. For example, young children intuitively know when they are finished eating. Their natural body wisdom— or prajna—is eventually bypassed because of being forced to finish the food on their plates. This often leads to habitual overeating in adulthood.

Prajnaparadha can also be instigated by frequent consumption of junk food and media. Nutrient-poor, empty-calorie, high-sugar foods desensitizes and confuses the body and brain. While the stomach may be full, hunger won't be satisfied as real nutrients are not sufficiently feeding the body. Therefore, frequent junk food eating frequently leads to overeating and addictive cravings. This phenomenon similarly occurs with the unsatisfying and addictive nature of excessive media.

Prajnaparadha also has an esoteric meaning. The word *aparadha* means to offend or go against our experience, true self-interest, and purpose. In Sanskrit, the word *apa* means to go against and *Radha* is pure love. Aparadha are unloving actions that cause harm to ourselves or others.

Continuously making negative choices due to ignoring our wise inner voice, perpetuates varieties of unhappiness, failure, addiction and even disease. Imbalance manifests to the degree we ignore our experience, innate intelligence and love. Cleansing has the amazing potency to reset and clear the body/mind palate. Therefore, clean eating, beneficial lifestyle practices and cleansing minimizes prajnaparadha and helps us attain our most significant goals.

Ama: The Secondary Cause of Disease

Ama, or toxins, can be externally generated, like pesticides in produce, or internally generated from improperly digested foods.

Internal Toxins

Internal toxins are compounds produced by your body. Excess hormones, undigested proteins, free radicals, bacteria, parasites and yeast are examples of internal toxins.

When internal toxins accumulate in the body, they can cause problems like inflammation, chronic infections, and allergic reactions.

External Toxins

External toxins are environmental toxins, externally produced but end up in our bodies. Pesticides and herbicides found in food, chemicals in cleaning and personal care products, heavy metals, mold, over the counter drugs, vaccines, are all externally generated toxins.

With an abundance of digestive issues and thousands of manufactured chemicals in our water and air as well as electromagnetic and wireless frequencies, it is no wonder our world continues to be challenged by cancer, autoimmune diseases, and anxiety disorders.

Buddhi: Innate Intelligence

Buddhi is the innate intelligence within all life. It manifests the laws of nature and controls the perfect rhythms and movements of the sun, moon, and tides. It's reflected in the interdependence of all kingdoms of life—microbes, plants, insects, fish, birds, animals, and humans. Buddhi enables cellular communication and the coordinated activity in our bodies that occurs without our conscious will. For example, we don't say, "Okay, now digest, please." Bodily processes happen automatically through the exquisite influence of buddhi. However, the healing influence of our innate intelligence can be obstructed by prajnaparadha and ama, or bad choices and toxins. When it is, the process of dis-ease can be initiated.

Prana: Vital Life Energy

Prana is the intelligent vitalizing life force. It's our electrical system within that energizes every cell of the body. Prana travels intelligently through channels known as nadis in ayurveda or meridians in acupuncture. Prana is subtle and influences both the body and mind. When it moves smoothly, we feel relaxed, alert, energetic, and enthusiastic, and our body and mind functions harmoniously. When it's imbalanced, our body and mind become disturbed. This appears as negativity, irritability, lethargy and physical discomfort. Prana manifests in five primary forms or directional flows of energy within our body: inward, upward, outward, around, and downward. Each prana supports specific functions on different levels of existence: physical, emotional, mental, and spiritual.

Agni: Fire of Digestion

Agni means "fire," and it relates to our metabolism and digestive power. It is that which consumes, assimilates, and transforms. Agni refers to the power of digestion and the capacity to transform food into the body's seven major tissues: plasma, red blood cells, muscle, fat, bone, marrow/nerves, and reproductive tissue. Many today, struggle with infertility. This can be due to having insufficient agni, as the body is unable to transform food and prana into healthy reproductive tissue.

When agni is sufficient, the body can efficiently release toxins, the senses and mind will be clear, and the energetic capacity to transform our lives in a positive direction will exist. When agni is deficient, dullness, heaviness, and stagnation of body, emotion and perception will be present.

Not only does agni transform the food we eat into our body, but it also transforms our sensory impressions and experiences into knowledge and wisdom. Everything we take in through our senses and mind—experiences, conversations, books, films, news, music, nature, social media—has to be digested, or assimilated, transformed, and understood with agni. Agni is also the fire of intelligence which gives us the ability to perceive and understand.

Ayurveda teaches that the original cause of mental or emotional imbalance is due to "undigested experiences". Some experiences are so overwhelming that they are "indigestible," at the moment they occur, such as serious trauma and abuse. Undigested experiences store in the nervous system, muscles, and organs. In time, they can derange the flow of vital life energy, leading to discomfort, pain, mental disturbance, and even disease. Therefore, it"s essential to cleanse and heal both body and mind!

Ojas: Essence of Immunity

Ojas is the essence of our immunity. It nourishes, strengthens, and gives endurance and longevity. Strong ojas provides physical wellbeing and a powerful will, mind and intellect. Ojas protects us from negativity, resists disease and enables us to recover after becoming ill. A sluggish lymphatic system, due to toxicity and poor diet causes stagnation and will interfere with the positive power of ojas. Cleansing, on many levels, strengthens ojas, and supports optimal immunity and health. An interesting note is that it is said that kindness and generosity actually strengthen ojas/immunity. The quality of ojas can be observed by the amount of luster of the eyes.

In Summary

Toxins cause cellular damage and stagnation in our lymphatic system. They interfere with our prana, agni, and ojas, inside and around the cells. When our cells are deprived of prana, vital life energy, they quickly oxidize, stiffen, and prematurely die. They lose innate intelligence (buddhi), their healthy DNA coding and messaging (agni), and their structural health (ojas). When cells completely lose intelligence, they go mad, and can become cancerous. Ama-toxins interfere with the body's innate intelligence. This deranges pranic energy flows. Deranged prana moves into the digestive tract, weakens agni-digestion. When our digestion malfunctions, internal toxins again damage prana, agni, ojas, and buddhi. Minimizing toxic exposure, clearing toxins and strengthening the channels of detoxification are essential to any authentic health program and necessary for high-level wellbeing.

According to Ayurveda, cleansing heals not only the body, but our mind and inner self as well. Therefore, its goal includes improved physical wellbeing along with a clearer mind and renewed spirit!

The Five Goals of Life

"The meaning of life is to find your gift. The purpose of life is to give it away."

Zig Ziglar

Previously I emphasized the worthy goal of high-level health and energy. When we use that energy to fulfill our goals and essential purpose in life we become fully satisfied. Ayurvedic wisdom teaches that all human beings share in common five primary goals of life. Awareness of these goals can empower us to utilize our precious life energy to live up to our greatest potential.

The Five Goals of Life:

Dharma: essential life purpose

Artha: basic needs

Kama: need for pleasure

Moksha: desire for freedom and spiritual liberation

Prema: our desire for unconditional and divine love

While all five goals are important, dharma is the root and doorway to fulfillment. Clarity about and fulfilling our dharma is an essential purpose of cleansing.

Dharma

We all desire to awaken to our full potential. To do so, we must act according to our true nature with integrity. This is called dharma. We all have a dharma, or essential purpose, that perfectly suits us.

Dharma is the foundation of satisfaction and empowers us to fulfill our most cherished goals.

Dharma is defined as the inherent quality in an object or person. For example, the dharma of fire is heat and light. Personal and spiritual growth begins with being authentic. The sacred text, Bhagavad Gita, articulates this point.

It is better to engage in one's own occupation, even though one may perform it imperfectly, than to accept another's occupation and perform it perfectly. BG 18.47

Paraphrased, it's better to be yourself imperfectly, than to try to be someone else, perfectly. We shine our own light better than anyone else can.

Dharma is dependent on four legs:

Satya: truth

Saucha: purity

Ahimsa: nonviolence (compassion)

Tapas: discipline

When all four legs are strong, the foundation of dharma will be stable. If any legs are weak the table will wobble or collapse. For dharma to fully manifest, all four legs must be sufficiently sturdy.

Satya: Truth

Satya means truth. Truth exists without effort and is sincerity at its best. It takes effort to manipulate an image of ourselves but it's easy to be ourselves. Truth has a health- sustaining influence. Authentic self-expression is based on accepting our true nature, with its gifts and limitations. Professional, personal and spiritual growth are dependent on truth, this first leg of dharma.

Saucha: Purity

Saucha means purity. Purity is the power to discriminate between what is good for us and what is not. It's the ability to let go of that which does not serve our dharma. The process of digestion is a good example. When we eat, the small intestine extracts nutrients and passes on the rest to be eliminated. Similarly, purity empowers us to accept those things that are beneficial and reject that which is not. Purity protects the body and mind by letting go of that which is toxic and accepting that which serves our purpose and wellbeing.

Ahimsa: Nonviolence

Ahimsa means non-violence. It is the power of compassion and is the foundation of dharma. Nonviolence means to restrain from actions that are harmful to ourselves and others. Focusing on the faults in others is harmful, to ourselves and others. Doing so we "ingest" the negative qualities that we focus on. Nonviolence is not weakness. One can be nonviolent, competitive and effective at the same time, especially if we have plenty of the next leg, discipline.

Tapas: Discipline

Tapas means discipline. Tapas indicates the fire-like, focused intensity that burns through obstacles to fulfilling our goals. Passing through this fire, like trials of adversity, we emerge brighter, clearer, and closer to reaching our goals. Discipline while ignoring the other legs of dharma: truth, purity, and compassion, is not dharma. Dharmic discipline means to act in alignment with the other legs. It takes discipline to eat well, work hard, and become successful. It also takes discipline to make time for fun, family, exercise, personal/spiritual growth, relationships and choosing compassion over selfishness.

Cultivating all four legs of dharma liberates a powerful source of internal energy that transcends ordinary human performance. Discovering and living our dharma is an ongoing process—it deepens and reveals itself in time. Eating clean, cleansing and following the above ayurvedic principles fosters the clarity of body and mind that guides us toward our dharma. When we are open and willing, life itself points us in the direction of our purpose. Our many "teachers", such as business, personal and spiritual mentors, relationships, nature and challenging experiences also help us to realize our calling.

I hope this chapter inspires you to live your purpose, fulfill your life goals, and attain extraordinary success, with integrity, wisdom and health in body, mind and soul.

***

websites:

www.healingessencecenter.com

www.totallifecleanse.com

https://mybodysite.com/jonathan-glass/total-life-cleanse

Total Life Cleanse book: https://amzn.to/3I5C7QU

https://healingessencecenter.com/product/the-book-total-life-cleanse/

Social Media:

Instagram : jonathanglass.m.ac

Facebook: https://www.facebook.com/JonathanGlass108

phone:

9783699228

Text:

9783448019

Prof. Olga Mroz

Prof. Olga Mroz, Dame of Honour is Professor and Director at OPEN WORLD and Art Business Program in Al-Khalifa Business School, the Editor and Chief of AKBS Journal. Professor Olga Mroz is Board Member delegate of Art and Culture of the Private Council of H.H. Prince Mahmoud Salah Al Din Assaf. She is International Golden Ambassador for Culture "BOOKS for Peace" and Global Ambassador CEC – "Commonwealth Entrepreneurs Club." She is a speaker, author, collector, and artist. Her paintings are in private collections around the world.

Based on the recommendation of the board of trustees and the governing council of the Asian African Chamber of Commerce & Industry she is an honorary member in the Board Advisors of the Asian African Chamber of Commerce & Industry.

Prof. Olga Mroz, Dame of Honour was born in Russia, and she has been living in Germany since 1992. She graduated in Architecture and Art, has degree in Theatre and Music by the Institute of Performing Arts of St. Petersburg. She also holds a degree in Artist Psychology by Art Academy of Moscow. She used to be a representative of many artists in Europe for many years, and she is dedicated to developing and managing various art projects now. The CIO TIMES Magazine recognized her as "THE MOST SUCCESSFUL BUSINESSWOMEN TO WATCH 2021."

Energy of Life

By Professor Olga Mroz

"I'm rich, I'm successful," I sang to the noise of the car's engine.

A warm light breeze touched my cheek, white curls developed in different directions, I squinted at the sun, hot rays burned my happy freckle-covered face. I was sitting behind the wheel of a red car, a huge bright sun shining from the back leather seat in a golden frame. I picked up speed, I was in a hurry! I am going to Paris!!! My Sun, my picture will be seen by the Louvre, the whole world will see!!! Happiness overwhelmed my heart!!! "I'll buy my mom a beautiful ruffle-toed dress. No, I'll buy her a nice hat because I have a lot of money, I'm rich."

My musings were interrupted by my sister's childish cheerful laughter, which pulled me out of my dream, my slumber. I stayed lying down, cozily wrapped in a blanket, I could still feel the sound of wheels sliding across the asphalt.

I had this dream when I was 14, a dream that changed my whole life. I had a goal to become successful, rich, and famous. Moreover, I had a great desire to bring joy and light to people with my paintings.

Let me introduce myself: I am a professor and director of the art business program at the International Business School, editor of the Art Journal. I am a delegate to the Arts and Culture Council of the Private Council of the Royal Family and an honorary member of the Council of Counsellors of the Chamber of Commerce and Industry in one of the regions of Africa.

I am a speaker, author, artist, and antique collector.

I'm successful, I'm rich, I'm happy!!!

May my example inspire everyone on the path to success and wealth.

Cracking The Rich Code!!!

My painting "Energy of life" today flew to another part of the globe. I still hear congratulations: "That is amazing dear Professor!"..., "You manage to combine the inspiring world with the wisdom from the academic world in this unity represents all good qualities that you pose and want to support in others" ..., "Great work dear Professor, "Energy of Life" mirrors the energy and life force you bring to the world with your talent"..., "Congratulations on a job well done!"...

I love the smell, the play, and the movement of colors. Brushstrokes, which allow me to describe my state of mind and express my feelings on canvas, have been familiar to me since childhood.

I organized my first exhibition of paintings at the entrance of our house when I was five years old. They were smiling suns with freckles on my cheeks and big rays like my mom's curls.

From early childhood, we knew what money was.

The topic of how to treat money and how to use it, Dad raised at every opportunity. He was very cautious and respectful of money. In the store, receiving a change of one penny, he always said - "A penny saves a money." He demanded the same thing from us. "When you start earning money yourself, then you will understand that money must be "saved". He tried to let us know that money would have an impact on our independent lives in the future.

When my sister and I started getting pocket money, he always wondered how much we spent and what we spent. One day my sister and I spent all the money on paints for drawing. We walked happy, dancing and whirling, home. I was already imitating the plot of my new painting. It was a special sun for animals in Antarctica. I wanted to save them from the cold. My sister dreamed of painting her shoes in a New Year's serpentine. What a disappointment it was when our parents condemned our act. The following month, instead of pocket money, we received a piggy bank.

Dad always saved some of the money, as he said, for a "rainy" day. I was 17 years old when we got the car. He saved money for it for 3 years. During these years, Dad made us less and less happy with gifts. Due to the restriction of family expenses, we stopped going on vacation with the whole family, we lost freedom of movement. For the first time, I realized that **Wealth is money** that can provide freedom and independence.

To dress beautifully and fashionably, I learned to sew and crochet clothes for myself and my sister. My sister and I were developing our children's models together, making patterns, and my mother taught us how to sew on a sewing machine. I was sewing my mother's old clothes in a new way. One day I spent money to buy fabric from which I made beautiful skirts for myself and my sister. The money was intended to pay for school lunches. For this action, we were both punished. My parents forbade us to sew throughout the week.

But I have already learned to get out of their difficult situations and not despair. My sister was adept at selling my paintings to neighbors and friends at school. Soon we had our finances and could buy beautiful fabrics to our liking. She kept a financial count. In the evening, when my parents came home from work, we had a fashion show. I loved those family evenings of ours. They were forever imprinted in my memory with the brightest moments of inspiration. Self-affirmation and the dawn of my childhood and adolescence. I hung my paintings on the walls, we put our new clothes, sewn by our own hands, and spun in a waltz. Mom and Dad could not resist such a festive atmosphere and danced with us. As I danced, I could see my suns vindicating ae with their rays and dancing with us. In those moments, I realized another meaning of the word **"Wealth" – it's family.**

My mom supported my creativity. It allowed me to use my talent in various ways. She often told me, "You're special, you're successful." This "Peculiarity" required a lot of discipline from me. I carefully prepared for lessons at school, I could not afford to be able to answer the teacher's question. I studied perfectly. I loved learning, reading a lot, and expanding my knowledge, and in books, I found answers to questions that interested me and to topics that weren't discussed in the classroom.

I was the soul of my classmates, and after organizing my solo exhibition at school, I gained credibility with my teachers.

After graduating from school, with great enthusiasm, I began to get acquainted and be interested in the works of other artists. One idea after another arose in my head. I needed a large field to implement them.

Having selected a group of artists whose paintings interested me and radiated positive energy, I organized a one-day exhibition for the sale of paintings on the street, since I did not have the means to pay for the premises. The paintings were held in the hands of the artists themselves. Although there was not a single sale of paintings, I received a great boost of energy for my further work. **"Wealth" is ideas**.

Success was not long in coming. I drew the attention of the press, and I received an invitation to prepare a project in a business firm. Having earned money, I immediately bought the paintings from the artists. That's how I got my first collection of paintings. Thanks to my self-confidence and opportunities, this exhibition has become the starting point of my long-term financial and creative success. **"Wealth" is self-confidence.**

I'm 18 years old. The older I got, the more I was interested in artists and history from different eras. Visiting museums and exhibition halls has become an integral part of my life. I tried to study more in the fields of art and culture. After graduating from the Faculty of Architecture and Art, I continued my studies at the Faculty of Theatre and Music Arts and received a degree in Artist Psychology from the Academy of Arts. I can confidently say that there is another meaning of the word **"Wealth" – it is knowledge**.

During my studies, I got married, we had a child. My husband worked, I worked with the child. It was difficult for us to live on my husband's salary alone. I worked part-time, sat with textbooks until late at night. For myself, I knew that to be a successful woman, in no case should you sacrifice your own family. If the word "victim" stands between family and career, it would be a fake success.

I started my long career as a director of musical theatre.

At the time, I was the only woman in this position. It was not at all easy to collaborate with well-known producers and directors. I even trained my voice to gain firmness, confidence, and clarity in tone. Every day I had to prove the correctness of my decisions. At the same time, I was faced with the problem of inequality between men and women in society. From my experience in theatre management, I have tried to prove that women can play a significant role in the economy.

With my activities and innovations that led to success, I was able to prove that women are important not only as employees but also in leadership positions.

Paying serious attention to the topic of" Gender Empowerment", I began to speak at various conferences, write articles on this topic. **"Wealth" is career.**

But the passion for painting did not leave me throughout my career. I enjoyed working with new young talented artists.

I was also interested in finding myself on canvas. I, like all artists, was looking for a new style of painting.

I was driven by a great desire to get acquainted with artists from different countries, as well as to show the world new, young, talented, not yet known artists. All my projects and exhibitions were aimed at the development of social and cultural innovations and were a great success. I have maximum financial freedom and independence. To ensure long-term and stable financial freedom, I began to invest part of my savings in the purchase of paintings, the value of which increased over the years. The demand for my paintings also increased, and the price increased accordingly. I began to increase my capital. Having defined my mission in business, I knew that I wanted to contribute to improving people's lives, to make the world brighter and more prosperous with equal opportunities for all. It became important for me to instill art, education, and culture in the younger generation and, of course, enjoy my work. This is a great task and a great responsibility. I was confident in myself and tried to prove my actions in concrete cases. **"Wealth" is to define a purpose in life.**

I often provided art paintings from my collection at auctions, participated in many charity events, and made a great contribution to helping children in need. On the back of every charity work I had in my painting of the Sun; I could feel the faces of the children smiling back at me. By helping, I gained more confidence that yes, I could be useful to society. Our planet is one big family where everyone should take care of their neighbor. You can't remain indifferent while there are so many injustices in the world: unequal access to clean drinking water, health care, education, and so on. I discovered another meaning of the word **"Wealth" - to be generous**

and help those in need. Each time I helped others, I became even richer and more successful.

As I put on exhibitions in different cities in Europe, I enjoyed and was inspired by the multicultural spirit and the freedom of creativity. I was glowing with happiness and overwhelmed with the energy I was rushing to reflect on canvas. On days like this, I painted the bright Sun. I loved to paint it since I was a child. On cold winter days, my sun-filled our room with its energy. I felt our mutual love, me and the sun were inseparable. But there have been cloudy days in my life. During the war in the Balkans, an exhibition of paintings that I organized was bombed. Those were years of civil wars. Although the insurance company paid the artists, it was impossible to compensate for the loss of the works of art created by the artists, and most importantly to restore them. At that time, I was not prepared for difficult situations, I did not have a strategy in the direction of preparing for problems.

It was only through my positive attitude in life and the confidence that my work and perseverance would help me achieve the greater professional success that I continued to go towards my goal. What's more, this situation has made me even stronger. A young dreamer with freckles turned into an independent strong woman with a firm character. I successfully sold my paintings on the international market. Along with this, I was already a professor and director of art programs at an international business school. **"Wealth" is a positive attitude.**

Given my heavy workload and activity in the business world, I could not do without a work plan. This made it easier for me to follow the progress of work, achievements, be flexible to changes, and most importantly save working time. "Time is Money"– I have often heard this brilliant phrase throughout my life, which was once uttered by Benjamin Franklin. If you learn how to properly distribute and use your time, not to waste it, then it will bear fruit.

While still a student, I received an invitation to take part in an art project at the university. On the way to the first meeting, I met a friend of mine whom I had not seen in a long time. She enthusiastically told me about her trip to the sea. As a result, I was 10 minutes late for the meeting. Imagine my surprise that the door was closed, and, on the door, I read the note of the project manager "I do not waste my time in the waiting rooms." I was at a loss at the time. A thought flashed through my mind, "I think I'm only 10 minutes late. He could have waited, I'm ready to apologize for my tardiness…" Unfortunately, I lost a good opportunity to participate in the project then. But that note on the door served as a good lesson for me in the future. I realized that time is precious, it must be used wisely, and be able to value not only your time but also the time of others. Another meaning of the word **"Wealth" is time.**

Yes, time moves inexorably forward. I sit in the garden of my house, swaying slightly in the rocking chair. I feel the early rays of the sun on my face, I enjoy a new day. Last night I flew in from the conference. I'm at the top of my career, I'm successful, I'm rich. I am grateful for my fate. But I want to look back at the beginning of my path, which I chose myself. It will not be fair if I say: "Me, me…" Throughout my career, my entire life path, I am accompanied by faithful and devoted friends, companions of my life. In my childhood, I thought that the whole world was my friends. With deep naivety, I drew pictures and sent them to different cities and countries, offering my friendship. I didn't get a response to my letters, but it didn't upset me.

The older I got, the more I became aware of the concept of friendship. I learned to understand and appreciate the selfless support of people close to me, not to be offended by their criticism or lack of time to meet with me. I am very grateful and infinitely happy that my friends were there when my husband died after a serious and prolonged illness. It was a difficult time for me, the loss of the closest and dearest person to me... The ground collapsed under my feet... I was confused, I didn't know how to react, how to become strong. I wanted to go back to my job, to paint again. But the forces left me, in my paintings, there was a dark sun, without rays.

After much persuasion, I went on a trip accompanied by friends. I was surrounded by care and warmth. Evenings were spent in meaningless conversations. But it was a call to Life. When I got home, I felt a surge of energy, I painted my picture. They were people dancing in the sun. They called me to life, to love. Yellow prevailed on the canvas. It is a bright, cheerful, embodying energy and movement color, familiar to me since childhood. I was determined to move in front. I wanted to shout to the whole world: **"Wealth" – these are my friends!**

Swaying slightly on the rocking chair, impressed by my memories of friends, I dozed off. " I stand on the stage among my dear friends, among successful business - people from all over the world. I have the Prize in my hands... I'm happy, I'm proud..." But it wasn't a dream. That's how yesterday at the conference went. Yes, I stood on stage yesterday among prominent people from all over the world. Passion, outstanding vision, values, investments, sustainability, education, new technologies, experience – all this has united us to improve the quality of life on outpour planet. I have been awarded for outstanding vision, dedication, and success along with extraordinary leadership and advisory skills, excellent cooperation, and support to Global Family and the Royal office. I was proud.

Yes, I cracked my Rich Code: "Energy of Life"!

Money, ideas, family, self-confidence, knowledge, time, purpose, generosity, career, positivity, friends – this is not a complete list that allowed me to become rich, successful, happy.

Each of us has his sun, his way, his chance. The most important thing is to confidently go forward. When we fall, we get up when we lose, we find. Every morning the sun rises, and the sun's rays give us the energy of life. "Energy of Life"- my picture today flew to another part of the globe to give people positive energy, the energy of life.

***

To contact Olga:
Website: http://akbs.assafdynasty.com
eMail.: o.mroz@akbs.assafdynasty.com
https://www.olgamrozgallery.akbseducationholdings.co.uk/discover-the-collection
LinkedIn: Prof. Olga Mroz, Dame of Honour linkedin.com/in/prof-olga-mroz-dame-of-honour-28728419b
Facebook: Olga Mroz
Instagram: olga.mroz.prof

Tristan and Melanie Helm

Tristan and Melanie Helm were raised in diverse backgrounds and had many adversities and hardships. They were linked in friendship and the adversities helped bond them in love. Tristan has worked in the mental health field helping individuals for almost 20 years and has a deep-rooted passion for helping people find the value inside of them. Coming from varying atmospheres, Tristan developed a strong desire for stability and self-awareness. As an author and speaker, Tristan has worked with many people aiding them to find their pathway by helping them to understand their past and helping them strengthen perspective and mental power. Melanie has worked in Wellness for over 10 years and feels it is her calling. By working through past traumas, she has a passion to guide others in breakthroughs to do the same. Together, they formed their business: Helm Mastery. They work with individuals to create a healthier, more balanced quality of life.

Rich in Spirit and Truth

By Tristan and Melanie Helm

Let me begin by asking, why do you want to be rich? Or better yet, why is being "rich" important to you? You picked up this book for a reason, and it is essential to define why it matters and what it means to you. When you take a step back and examine the motives and reasons for why you want something, it can help you take much larger steps later, or even push past moments where you question yourself as to why you started this journey to begin with. There are very few certainties in life, but knowing why and where you are going can help increase the chances of it happening. It also helps when you set your sights on the things that truly matter, and will endure past anything materialistic, which are ultimately connected to spirituality and truth.

The purpose of this chapter is not to persuade you into a religion; it is merely to broaden the perspective that few things matter more than these. Truth is relevant and thus grounded in facts, and your spirit, the soul inside your body, will last forever. I did not choose this topic to win anyone to my belief in Christ. While I do stand firm that is of the utmost importance for my family, I do not seek to change anybody's mind. I intend to just present the facts and pray that those that are willing to listen here. While this chapter may have scriptures, it is not about Christianity. This chapter is just meant to open up the eyes of those willing to look for something more. This chapter is about being rich in the spirit and being rich in what is true.

Genesis 2:7 says, "the Lord formed man of the dust of the earth, and breathe into his nostrils the breath of life, and Man became a living soul." When my father died in 2020, it broke me and as I was grieving next to his bed, I looked up and saw that his weight had changed since when he was brought in. The screen that was monitoring him flashed big bold letters "Weight differs from original weigh-in". Essentially it was saying that my father was weighing substantially less than when he was brought in. The only difference was that he was no longer breathing, and his heart had stopped; his organs remained intact, he had not lost any blood, and nothing had changed. You could also feel the temperature drop in the room. My father's spirit had left his body. Now whether we want to admit it or not, there is a part of us that wants to last forever. There is substantial evidence that supports man has a soul. While it takes faith to believe this, there is enough evidence to suggest that we are not merely particles and atoms. I have been seeking and growing in spiritual truth for the past 18 years, but I have never felt or seen anything like what I experienced in that hospital room the day my father died.

The Things That Last

Money is exchanged or fades. Objects and materials collect dust or even get destroyed and lies are eventually surfaced and found out. But the spirit and absolute truth, based on facts, they are timeless and foundational. They stay the same, despite all the changes that go on in the world. Think of the legends that have passed before us and how what they stood for or the differences that they make have surpassed the death that took them from this world. How they lived and what they said lived much longer than their lives allowed. Being rich is much more than materialistic things. It's more than a dollar amount or anything that we might hold dear and treasure in our lives covetously.

There must be more than what is in front of us, more than the glamour, more than fame, more than quantifiable riches that we would hold with our hands or in the banks. If that's all there is for life, it is meaningless. One of the richest men in the world of all time (around 2 trillion dollars in today's amount), Solomon once said "I have seen all the works which have been done under the sun, and behold, all is vanity, a futile grasping and chasing after the wind (Ecc 1:14).

While there is nothing wrong with wanting money, and desiring to be wealthy, it is not all there in life. It's a vain and expendable accolade. It would be the equivalent of getting a car, just so you could get more gas. Money is a tool, something to be used to obtain or take care of a priority. If your goal is to make money, ask yourself, what it is for? Why do you need it? What purpose does it place in your life? This is why we pursue things much more than that. If it needs the financial resources, so be it, but look beyond the tool and see what it could be used for.

When we look for the things that last, when we decide to pursue what will live beyond us, we begin a whole different life than we imagined before. Something magical opens up inside of us, we become adamant about the things that matter when we look for the truth and resurrect the spirit inside of us to think and be more. It is like our mind and myopic view of things reprioritize themselves and become focused on these things

Being rich is about prospering past hardships and having an abundance that can flow into other people. Simply put, the poor are much more than lacking things in this world. People have won the lottery, millions upon millions of dollars, and because of their mentality and the way they lived, went right back to where they were. People, who have instant success, according to the world standards of it anyways, are usually driven back to their reality when they have not adjusted properly to the required lifestyle that comes with it. That's why you can give the same thing to two different people when will take it and grow and the other one will either use it or forget all about it. It is not the objects we hold in our hands but rather the things that we place in our spirits that tend to last.

A Look into Spirituality

Spirituality is much more profound than going to church, temple, or an ashram; it's more than ushering or being a part of an auxiliary church function or group of like-minded people. It is a deep connection from your soul to the Divine and increases your capabilities. It ultimately is a choice we are all given the freedom to make where we go with it. Your spirituality is just taking the blinders off the world in front of you and looking to another dimension, whether it is through meditation or prayer, it is an experience to what is beyond the somatic realm. Some find it in their religion, some through yoga, and others look into just a close walk with God. What is most important is that you find the connection personally and you link your soul to something beyond you. It doesn't come easy, and can be very difficult and disheartening at times, but it can also take you to another place in life that nothing else can. Your soul is essential to the higher quality of life; it should be nourished and allowed to be enhanced.

The Search for Truth

"The truth shall set you free" John 8:32. Whether you are a follower of Jesus or not, there is something so fatefully true about it. Think of a time when you were so set in your ways on some topic, or a time when you held onto something dear to you until truth peered through the doors of life and opened. Perhaps you experienced something tragic, and the things you held onto and believed were vital, seemed trivial afterward because you saw the things you took for granted before. Perchance, you had a certain way things were done and you refused to try it another way, until someone you admired, came in and showed you a better, and this one new approach revolutionized the way you did it from that point. No matter the experience, your perspective opened up and you saw the world a little differently, it set you free, in some way. That's what this chapter is all about.

There is, at times, a vast difference between what is real and what is true. Truth is grounded in the facts while reality is based upon the way we see things through our perspective. Everyone, including the authors in this book, lives according to the perspectives and the biases they have in life. That is why people view things differently and responds in varying ways.

The reality in which we live is solely based upon this. Your mind cannot differentiate between what is true and what is not, so your body is going to respond the same as long as it perceives it as real. Seeking after the truth is not easy, being rich and what is true requires sacrifice and giving up comfort, but its reward will pay dividends and play a crucial role in the decisions that you make. When you seek truth, you're not seeking things that help you feel better about what you already believe, but rather the facts and the foundation that they hold. When you seek truth you are not swayed by emotions but rather directed by those foundations. Truth is more than numbers; it's beyond just the facts and the figures, the truth just looking objectively at something before making a decision.

Dream On

"Most people die at 25 and aren't buried until 75" Benjamin Franklin. While that quote is not found in any of the major work he is attributed for saying that. Regardless of who said it, it still rings true today. Life is more than just living and breathing, it is about the impact that we leave in this world. I would hold on to the theory that men die at 25 because they stop dreaming. They stop pursuing something that is out there in this world, and they just settle for what they have. Science shows a relative halt in new brain growth in activity around the age of 25 because all of the important stages that an individual has gone through have culminated to that point. In theory, from birth until that age, virtually everything is a learning experience but once someone settles into their comfort and their lifestyle, their brain stops developing.

Is there something brewing in your mind, an image you had of how things could be if only you took a step out, took a chance, and materialized it? Is there something you dreamt about as a kid that you kept to closer and more personal as you grew up, and now it is just a faded memory or something that died out? Life throws us off course and hands us challenges that disrupt our patterns of thinking and interrupt our dreams. We had a dream or a passion as a kid, and half expected things to run relatively smoothly until life took a swing and knocked us down, and kept coming at us until we surrendered our ambitions and settled for complacency and a sense of "normal"

Henry David Thoreau was quoted to say, "most men live in quiet desperation and go to the grave with the song still in them." I would dare to ask why. Why do we give up so easily? Why do we allow life to bring us to a halt when there is so much more ahead of us than what is behind us? Surely, age has very little to do with our purpose, when it happens, or even when we die. People have done things before their legal age of adulthood, as well as others, have done things well after the normal age of retirement. There is no way to determine whether we have measured up to our potential or have passed our time. The things that grow in our spirits are the things that cause the change this world needs. There can be a longing for what is good, and the love that yearns to be shared.

If you once had a dream, something that burned in your mind as a child, a pang of hunger in your spirit, a longing desire in your soul, I tell you NOW is the time to open that backup. Dream again. Get back on the court and challenge life to swing again. Take the hits and get back up. Get knocked down, stand up, and charge at it again.

Your spirit, your life, possibly others are depending on it. What if the world could be better if you dream again? What would you do if you could spend more time meditating and investing in your spirit with this dream?

The fanatical ones, the ones that refuse to die out, the ones that will not be silent or keep to themselves, are the ones that change this world. The ones that hold the truth in their heart and refuse to conform to social norms are the ones that become the legends among us. The ones that will not stand down won't be easily swayed or the ones that end up swaying others. Dream for yourself and dream for others. In the words of Schwartz from "A Christmas Story" I TRIPLE DOG DARE YOU! I dare you to dream, to live, to dig deep into your soul for that longing once again and dream.

The Paradox of Giving

It seems almost counterintuitive to talk about giving in this book. We're supposed to be increasing wealth not decreasing, right? I would like to propose something that seems almost uncanny. A multitude of the great minds in the world even those that have gone before us had tapped into a universal law. This is a biblical principle that so many have utilized to help build their wealth and create a more fulfilling life, even to find their true purpose. Two well-known individuals Tony Robbins and Dave Ramsey (both having a net worth between hundreds of millions and billions of dollars each) live their life and coach others by this principle. When you find a cause greater than yourself to give to it opens up a door in your life for you to receive more. You cannot receive from a closed fist. So when our hands are open and ready to give what we've been blessed with we are positioned to receive abundance.

You may have heard the term give and it shall be given unto you... This principle is written with time. In the Bible, it talks about bringing a tithe offering into the storehouse so that the things of God and those working the temple can be supported. So whether you get involved in your local church, you find a charitable cause, or maybe start a foundation of your own to help others in need remember it is more blessed to give than to receive.

Being truly rich

Ultimately you get to choose what you do in this life. You don't get the choice of what life throws at you, or get to decide what challenges you face, but you do get to make the decision on how you respond. You will get tired; you will want to give up. Life is going to shake you, you will be ridiculed, and things will get ugly at times. I promise it will not be easy, but it will be worth it. You will feel alive again. If you refuse to settle for less than what is out there, and not allow yourself the danger of being comfortable, you will find things in this life are more alive and rich than before.

Like I said at the beginning of this chapter, there are a few things that matter more in this world than what is true and the soul that is inside of you. You can choose your perception. You can value only the things in your immediate world, or you can do something about it. You can broaden your perspective and seek after the things that bring peace in your life and others. You can make it an investment into your spirit, and you can seek truth and not comfort. You can look for the things that don't make you happy but give you a sense of peace and fulfillment through the truths that you speak into life. Your life will reflect what you value and what you believe, much more than what you think. You have the power within you. You can create and be the change that this world needs. When you seek truth and you dream with your soul, and you live in that spirit, you become rich beyond your wildest dreams

Author/Speaker/ Perspective Coac
"Sometimes people just need a small adjustment in their life to go an entirely different direction" - Tristan Helm

***

To contact Tristan & Mealnie:

Email: helm105402@gmail.com Tristan@helmmastery.com

Phone: 682-233-4636

Web sites: www.helmmastery.com www.finding-yourbeauty.com

Facebook:
https://www.facebook.com/Helm_Mastery101882018132167/?mo dal=admin_todo_tour

Facebook Mental Group:
https://www.facebook.com/groups/701115637362940

Instagram: https://www.instagram.com/helm_mastery/

LinkedIn: https://www.linkedin.com/in/tristan-helm-2b60675b/

Martha Krejci

Do you know anyone that has gone from being an exhausted and undervalued mom in the corporate 9-5 world to a work from home powerhouse in the blink of an eye? Now let's add without a college degree and without ads... Well now you do!

Martha Krejci is a high-vibin' mama, wife, business coach + growth strategist and social media marketing powerhouse who has taken the internet by storm. Featured in Fox, ABC and CBS news, Oprah Magazine, Fast Company, Cosmopolitan, Shape and Huffington Post among other places, Martha's intuitive marketing expertise has helped her change the trajectory of her family's life in less than a year using a strategy she teaches openly through courses, group coaching and other tried-and-true resources.

She is now also on the Forbes Business Council. From finding your passion to building a business from home that works, she teaches it all to anyone that's ready.

How To Build A Multi-Million Dollar Business From Home Without Ads

By Martha Krejci

Have you ever had a seemingly innocent experience that changed everything? Like in a movie where the hallway gets narrow, the picture turns sideways, and you know that the character will never be the same? That's how it was for me.

Having my daughter was by no means effortless. There were many tests, injections, and painful let downs before those two pink lines appeared on that pregnancy test. My husband, Mike, and I were thrilled to be parents. I was the main breadwinner, so he stayed home with our daughter while I went back to work.

Time stops for no one, and I was no exception. I'll never forget the day that changed everything. I wasn't allowed to use my phone on the floor at work, so when I got a video message from my husband, I went to the bathroom to watch it. I stood in front of the sink as I played the video and watched my daughter take her first wobbly steps toward the camera. What I experienced next was simultaneous excitement that she was walking along with soul crushing heartbreak that I was missing it.

I watched my face crumple in the bathroom mirror as the heaviness threatened to consume me. Why had I fought so hard to be a mom if I was just going to miss every milestone and feel too exhausted to enjoy motherhood? Was this what I had to look forward to? Watching my daughter grow up through video clips my husband sent me because I wasn't there?

That was the day that I decided I was done. I got home and told my husband that I was quitting my job. God bless that man because he told me that I *had* to do it for every person I would impact. It was terrifying, though. I was supporting not only my family but also my husband's parents, who were living with us at the time. If I failed, we were all going down.

I immediately threw myself into learning everything I could from others who claimed to be able to teach me what I needed to know. I mean, how hard could it really be to build a successful business from home, right? What I quickly learned was that these "charlatans" didn't have the results they claimed to and that the way they were making money wasn't something I was willing to duplicate. It's not that I wasn't capable of doing it their way, but if I wanted to live with myself and not feel gross and slimy, I was out.

This left me in a challenging position, to say the least. How was I supposed to learn from the so-called "gurus" if what they were teaching didn't align with who I was as at my core? I didn't want to compromise my values just to make a few bucks.

I knew there had to be a better way, but I wasn't finding it. All I could think to do was create it myself. If the people I was trying to learn from weren't going to share what it really took to succeed from home, I was determined to figure it out and then equip others to do the same thing.

And that's exactly what I did.

Through trial and error — lots of error — I developed my own system over the course of a good decade. I was told by many people that I would never have the success I desired by showing up in service the way I wanted to. Basically, if I wanted to serve people, impact them in a profound way, and keep my prices accessible, I'd be broke. If I was willing to cheat people, stop caring about impact, and charge tens of thousands of dollars for my stuff, then, sure, I'd make it. But at what cost? I wasn't willing to find out.

I pulled skills from every position I'd ever had. For example, my job as a waitress/bartender equipped me with problem solving skills, the ability to think quickly on my feet (have you ever dealt with hangry people?), organizational skills, and the ability to stay cool under pressure and treat people kindly, even when they didn't reciprocate. What I found by working with the public in different capacities was that what people really needed was purpose.

Purpose was what I had been missing by working a desk job day after day. The '70s carpeted cubicle just didn't quite motivate me enough to get out of bed each day. What I needed was to feel like I was part of something bigger than myself. I needed to know that what I was doing would impact others in a positive way. I had to believe that my actions would leave this world a better place for my daughter. It turns out, a lot of people felt the same way.

I discovered that all people really needed was to be shown what to do by someone who knew what they're talking about. I've been able to change the entire trajectory of my family's life by building multiple income streams from home on five to ten hours per week. Do you want to know my secret sauce? It's probably not what you think it is.

The secret sauce is … (drum roll, please)—community.

I have become a master at building community with my people. I focus on giving away massive value for free, building trust, and supporting people however I can. I invest in my people far sooner than they ever invest in me. That's what I live by, and that's how I choose to do business. If it's not a win-win-win, then I'm not interested. I believe this is why I've been able to garner the level of loyalty that I have. It's why people like me, trust me, and want to keep doing business with me. I show up for them because it's why I was put on this earth. I believe that with every fiber of my being.

You might be asking yourself "*how* do I do this", and that's totally fair. Let's talk about some practical things that I do regularly.

First, I nurture people. What that looks like practically is showing up live on social media every weekday for fifteen minutes to pour into them. I give practical, helpful tips that they can implement immediately, and I do it all for free. Doing this consistently does a few different things. It lets people know that I'm not going anywhere. They know they can depend on me to be there day in and day out, and that builds trust. It also overdelivers. I'm not showing up live and withholding value from them so that they have to buy something from me to get anything out of it. I give them gold that they can use right away because, like I said, I invest in them long before they invest in me. If they decide that the next logical step is to jump into one of my programs, then, great!

Another thing that showing up live does is give people a chance to get to know me. They see how I talk, how I teach, what I laugh about … They hear the inflection of my voice as I get passionate about a topic, and because my people are just like me, they connect with and align with me. They know I'm their person and that I'm here for them specifically. The only way to make sure that happens is to show up consistently. You can't expect to build a tribe of loyal people by just throwing ads at them. You've got to show up and do the work.

Spending money on ads is like throwing spaghetti at the wall and hoping that something will stick. It doesn't build trust or loyalty with anyone, and if they do end up buying what you're selling, they likely won't be retained as a client. I'm really good at ads. In fact, some would even call me an ads guru. It's what I did professionally for many years. I know how to write a good ad and sell a product. If that was my end goal, then, I'd be happy. My end goal is not a sale, though; it's impact.

If I can't build trust and loyalty with someone, I can't impact them. I can't help them be better. I can't help them move the needle on their business and their life. All I can do is sell something and hope they like it. That's not how I choose to do business, and I hope it isn't how you choose to do business either.

The next thing I do daily is reach out to people on Facebook messenger. Before you roll your eyes and think to yourself, "There it is — the thing I won't be comfortable doing ...", hear me out. I don't message people to sell them stuff. There are no "hey, girl, hey" messages that will ever come from my inbox to yours. That's not who I am, and that's not what I teach people to do. If I can also digress for a moment here, please don't send those messages either. When you send your list of friends a "hey, girl, I thought of you for my new biz and just knew you'd be amazing at it. When's a good time to talk?" message, it's gross. I am positive you don't mean to come off that way, but it's just what we're taught, isn't it? "Send a message to everyone you know because it's just a numbers game." How about we stop treating people like a number, m'kay? This isn't some kind of game. This is about people's lives and freedom.

So now that that's out of the way, let's talk about what I actually do with Facebook messenger. Every day, I message five to ten people on my friends list to say hi and see how they're doing. That's it. I know; it's shocking, isn't it? I don't message people with the intention of selling them something or backing them into a hard close conversation. The reason I message people every day is twofold. First, it's to connect with them. I genuinely want to know how they're doing and how they've been. In the kind of culture we live in today, that kind of thing is needed now more than ever.

The other reason I message people daily is because it's an algorithm hack. Say what? Did you think I was just getting all touchy feely on you and wasn't going to give you business tips? I've got you! You see, when you have conversations with people in Facebook messenger, it tells Facebook that your content needs to be seen by more people. All of a sudden, more people start to see your videos, your posts, and your content, and that helps you have a bigger impact. It's a win-win, and you know how I feel about those.

Everything I do is about reaching back into the fire and pulling others out. When I was in that cubicle, I felt trapped. I was afraid that I would miss out on my daughter's whole life — all of those moments that I would miss because I was at work, all of that time I would never be able to get back. I spent my days wondering if there was more to life than what I was living. I longed to make a difference in people's lives, but I had no idea where to start. I was desperate to make an impact but wasn't sure if anyone would ever listen to a divorced former alcoholic. My track record wasn't exactly one of success.

If you've been feeling the same way, you're not alone. I believe that every person on the planet has a unique calling on their life that only they can fulfill. I believe that the only reason we go through a difficult circumstance is so that we can turn around and help others through the same thing. This is what I do. I show people how to make a massive impact in the lives of the very people they feel called to serve. I show them how to monetize multiple streams of income using their passions.

Just like my student, Meggan Larson, who was making $3.45/hour — seriously, that's not a typo. She had been trying and failing for thirteen years to make an income from home. She was working for someone who continually asked more and more of her to the point that she was working forty to sixty hours per week. Her impact moment came when she realized that her son had stopped asking her to read to him. She asked him why, and his words broke her heart,

"You always say no, Mommy. You're always too busy, so I stopped asking."

Ouch!

She jumped into my coaching, and within a few short months, she had quit her job, retired her husband, had way more time with her kids, and more savings in the bank than ever before.

My student, Danelle Fowler, had been working in corporate America, feeling like life was being drained from her. It was a high stress job that left her with a form of PTSD. After jumping into my coaching, she quit her job, started a new career from home, and is thriving.

My student, Lauren da Silva, was burned out, to say the least. She was at the point where she just wasn't sure if life was ever going to get any better. She now has a successful coaching program and was just invited to be a keynote speaker at a local event in April for struggling women entrepreneurs. Those are the very people she feels called to helped.

I could go on and on — literally, I have thousands of testimonials just like these. What I want to impart to you is that it's possible. Whatever your dreams are, they're possible. That nagging feeling that you get when you're all alone, telling you there has got to be more to life than what you're living, is there for a reason. It's there to make sure that you stop settling. You were never meant to be tied to a job that would replace you in a second if they needed to. You were never meant to live a life of mediocrity just so that you could afford to pay the bills. There's so much more to life than that.

I was an alcoholic bartender living in a friend's basement at one point. If I can go from that space to changing the trajectory of my entire family, then so can you. I found the courage to step out in faith and with the determination to make sure I didn't quit until I reached the success I was after.

I won't leave you behind.

If you are feeling the nudge that there's more for you than what you're currently living, then I'm your person. I put the easy button on creating multiple high profit income streams from home. I'm not just going to cheer you on, get you excited, and then leave you hanging. I will take you step-by-step to where you want to go, the same way I've done for thousands of others.

Grab my free guide – How To Quit Your Job Without Going Broke, Even If You Have No Skills. marthaekrejci.com/quit Like I said before — I invest in you long before you ever invest in me. I believe in you, and I would love to link arms with you and impact the world together.

You in?

***

To Contact Martha:

Website: www.withmartha.com

Instagram: www.instagram.com/themarthakrejci

Facebook: https://www.facebook.com/martha.krejci1111

YouTube: www.watchmartha.com

LinkedIn: https://www.linkedin.com/in/themarthakrejci/

Joe Nunziata

Joe Nunziata is a best-selling author, spiritual life and business coach, and professional speaker who teaches that to make permanent changes you must clear your negative energy and break destructive patterns of behavior at the core level. The transformational process that Joe developed enables people to create new energy and beliefs designed to achieve sustained, positive growth in all areas of life.

The career that Joe has created for himself is not something most would expect from a Brooklyn-born son of a New York police detective and conservatively thinking mother. After losing his father at the age 12, Joe felt he had to become the man of the family. He worked and struggled for years before realizing he had to deal with his issues from the inside to make lasting changes.

Since 1992, Joe has been delivering his life-changing message at events and seminars. His programs blend spirituality, psychology, philosophy and the power of internal energy. He has appeared on many television and radio programs including Good Day New York and Street Talk on Fox TV, Cablevision News 12, Gaiam TV, Better TV, The Braveheart Network and various radio shows, podcasts, and summits worldwide.

Joe's work led him to author several books, including, *Heal the Deal, Chasing Your Life, Karma Buster, Spiritual Selling, Finding Your Purpose and No More 9 to 5*. He has created many audio, video and written programs including, Elevate Your Energy Elevate Your Life, No More Mental Barriers, Connecting to Your Spirit and The 7 Keys to Transformation.

Elevate Your Energy, Elevate Your Life

7 Steps to Freedom

By Joe Nunziata

You are working hard, setting goals, doing affirmations, reading books, going to seminars, and signing up for coaching programs. After all this energy, effort, and investment, you find yourself sighing and asking…why isn't this working? I know the feeling very well.

I chased success for many years, following all the steps laid out for me by the experts. 'Was this a waste of time?' you ask. No way! Everything I learned and experienced moved me to a higher place. Finally, I was ready to receive the missing pieces of the puzzle that helped me turn my life around. To my great surprise, this was not about working harder or learning a new technique. Discovering how to make powerful internal shifts in my energy field is what made all the difference in my life.

My working career started at the age of 18 in Brooklyn, NY. After losing my father, a narcotics detective in New York City, at the age of 12, life took a dramatic turn. I was the oldest boy in an Italian Catholic family. It was important for me to go to work and start earning money. Although I did not have the opportunity to go to college, I was driven to improve myself and become a success. My belief system was simple back then; if I wanted to succeed, I had to work like a demon and keep moving forward. This philosophy took me on a wild ride of ups and downs—mostly downs.

After going through two bankruptcies by age 30, I knew something had to change. I could not understand why all of my hard work and determination was not paying dividends. Out of pure desperation, I decided to see a psychologist. This was not the path taken by Italian kids from Brooklyn, in my generation. I began with trepidation, but quickly became enamored with psychology and human behavior. My therapist gave me books to read and audio sessions to deepen my knowledge base. I could not get enough of this information. The fog was lifting, and I was beginning to see my life from an entirely new perspective.

This led me into metaphysical energy work. I started to study eastern philosophies, spiritual principles, meditation, and the power of energy vibration. Along my journey, I have met amazing friends and teachers—including medium John Edward and an enlightened master named Susan Kerr who told me I had blocked Chakras. I wasn't sure what that meant at the time, but it gave me quite a scare.

If you are not familiar with Chakras, they are energy points in your body that run from the base of your spine to the crown of your head. This is where you hold your internal energy. 'Chakra' is a Sanskrit word that means wheel. Energy cycles through your body and creates your vibration.

I then learned the key to making lasting changes in life. It had nothing to do with working hard or having the best sales pitch. The key was working from the inside out. This was a huge shift for a person like me, who had been conditioned to focus on material success and the trappings of the physical world. I learned to turn my attention inward to face my deepest issues and fears. The rest of this chapter will be dedicated to giving you tools to make this amazing transition in your own life. I will share my experience, as well as tools that have benefited me and thousands of others I have worked with over the last 30 years. All I ask is that you keep an open mind to a different way of thinking and seeing the world. When you choose this path, you are taking the high road, and we all know the high road is the hard road.

7 Steps to Freedom

Everything in life is based on energy. Your patterns, beliefs, blocks, cycles, and karma are all tied to your vibration of energy. This work is emotional, spiritual, and scientific. See yourself as pure energy instead of in physical form. As energy, you are vibrating at a certain frequency. This frequency goes out into the world and begins attracting things into your life. In addition, this same vibration is also repelling things. This is the basis for the law of attraction.

Following this logic, if you want to create a different outcome in life, you must change your frequency—the same way you would change stations on a radio to the music you prefer. If you love rock and roll, why would you tune into a jazz station? This may sound simple, but most people go through life on the wrong station and never realize it. You may ask, "How is that possible?" This goes back to your original programming and karma. I will address these issues to help create a clearer picture. You came into this world with karma based on the emotional issues you chose to explore and experience in this lifetime. To elevate yourself I am going to ask you to please remove logic from the equation. Your brain wants things to make sense. This is emotionally based work that will not make logical sense. If you are the type of person who loves everything to make logical sense, this will be challenging. Expansion requires leaving the box of logic and opening yourself to new possibilities.

Based on your karma, you made specific choices before you arrived here in physical form. You selected your gender, parents, where to be born, emotional traits and specific skills. By making these selections you created your DNA. This is the perfect combination of elements for your unique journey.

It is helpful to see this as a journey of discovery. You require issues, problems, and disruptions to have your selected experience. I can just hear all those logical people now, "Why in the world would I choose this path?" Allow yourself to accept that you made these choices and be open to new possibilities. This will help you move through your obstacles faster and with less judgment.

Step 1: Understanding Your Emotions and Beliefs

Your life is being created by your emotions and beliefs…not your actions. This can be a difficult pill for people to swallow. We have been conditioned to believe that if we want to accomplish something, it is critical to take massive action. This philosophy was at the center of all my problems. Let me be clear regarding action. I am not saying action is unnecessary, but not all action is created equal.

It is all a matter of alignment and flow. When you are in good energy, and follow your feelings, you are taking inspired action. This action is tied to your true desires and highest self. Conversely, when you take actions tied to negative emotions and fears, you are out of alignment. In this negative state, it is impossible to create long-term positive results.

Step 2: Identify Your Negative Cycles

All things happening in your life are tied to cycles of energy. These cycles are occurring all day long in all areas of your life. They are present in your relationships, career, health, and financial condition. Understanding these cycles opens the door to positive change.

Most of us have been conditioned to problem solve as a mode of change. If plan A does not work, you move on to plan B. These adjustments take place on a surface level. We have been conditioned to react to the outside world. We believe we did something wrong or there was some outside issue causing the problem. Thinking this way traps your brain in an endless loop of problem solving to find an answer in the outside world. There is no way to move forward because you are looking for the answers in the wrong place. The key is identifying your emotional cycle and breaking it at the core level.

Take a few minutes to identify your cycles of behavior, and their results, in all areas of your life. I remember doing this many years ago with a yellow legal pad. Because I am anal, I placed the year next to each event and created a chronological list. This was a truly amazing exercise. I saw the exact sequence of both of my bankruptcies in writing. It was sobering and liberating at the same time.

Step 3: Changing Your Perspective

In most cases people are only able to see what is directly in front of them and act accordingly. Making core changes requires you to see things from a higher perspective. True change occurs on an emotional level. It is an adjustment to move to a new perspective after years of seeing things a certain way.

I have encountered this many times working with corporations. They see the numbers and productivity, but not the people. Most people are unhappy at work because they do not feel valued or appreciated. It has nothing to do with money. The negative cycle and high turnover are tied to how people feel. Getting corporations to understand this concept can be challenging.

A few years back, we were taking a long car trip. I needed new sunglasses and went to the mall. There was a kiosk selling all types of sunglasses. The guy asked me how I would be using them. I told him it was for a driving trip. He directed to me a pair that was designed to cut glare on the road. These were, of course, more expensive than the basic version. I asked what made these better. He proceeded to give me the basic pair, then asked me to look at a frame that was hanging on the outside of his kiosk. It was a black frame with white paper on the inside. "What do you see?" he queried. I said, "Nothing, just a blank piece of white paper." He then handed me the more expensive pair that was designed for driving. When I looked at the frame a second time, a dragon appeared. Where did it come from?

These new glasses gave me the ability to see something I could not see before. The irony: the dragon was always there. I just needed the right glasses to see it. This is what happens when you see things from a higher place. You are not reacting to what is happening in the physical world, as you now know the truth is hiding in a higher place.

Step 4: Identifying Your Emotional Anchors

Everything is energy, and you are vibrating at a frequency that is creating your life. It is important to readjust this frequency at a core level to achieve lasting positive changes. People struggle because they are not getting to the core of the issues causing their pain. It is easier to go for a quick fix and our society pushes that agenda— taking prescription drugs and going for weight loss surgeries instead of working on a better lifestyle and diet. The list goes on and on.

You are going to become empowered and that means rolling up your sleeves to create lasting changes you can build upon. Your emotional anchors are tied to incidents that occurred when you were a child. The emotional trauma of these incidents created energy that you continue to replay. These are the issues you came to resolve. As I said earlier, you chose your situation to recreate these issues and clear the karma. Identifying these emotional anchors opens the door to healing yourself.

Here is an example of how it works:

Joan has been an executive assistant for many years. Her boss is very demanding and always makes her feel she is not doing enough. This is the energy she has always carried, and as a result, she continues to attract people who do not appreciate her in all areas of life. When Joan gets upset, her default behavior is to make an excuse for her boss, or anyone else who mistreats her. She cannot accept the truth and this denial keeps her in the cycle.

The question to ask yourself is, 'how does this make me feel?' In Joan's case, she was feeling unloved and unappreciated. Those are the true emotions. Next question: who made you feel this way growing up? This will usually tie back to one or both of your parents or a primary caregiver you had growing up. Joan tied these emotions back to her father.

By not dealing with this emotional issue, Joan is holding the energy and recreating the same cycle. Once you identify the emotion, and person who caused it, you are ready to clear the energy.

Step 5: Clearing the Energy

Energy is cleared when you allow yourself to feel the pain of the emotions you have been blocking. Instead of feeling the emotions, Joan has been defending the perpetrator and making excuses for the behavior. Accepting the truth is painful, which is why we avoid these emotions.

I learned to clear my energy using a meditation process. Sit quietly and bring a recent incident into your mind. Let's say Joan's boss insulted her in front of her coworkers. As she replays the incident in her mind, it brings up the feelings of being unloved and unappreciated. She must go back to where it came from—her father. Now, Joan will allow herself to feel the anger she has towards her father and the emotional pain she felt. As she is feeling these emotions, the energy she was holding is released, allowing it to leave the Chakra System of the body. Once the energy is cleared, Joan's energy frequency is changed. You can also clear the energy any time you have the awareness and feel the emotion. I find the meditation helps me get on a deeper level.

Note: It may take several meditations to fully clear deeper emotional issues. Some will be cleared quickly, while others will take more time. In any case, every time you feel the emotion, you are clearing energy and elevating.

You can dig deeper into this process with my full *Elevate Your Energy, Elevate Your Life* program. See details at http://elevateyourenergynow.com

Step 6: Adjusting Your Energy

Every time you clear energy by feeling a blocked emotion, your physical body has to adjust to the new higher vibration. This is a process you will repeat over and over again. Your physical body removes the dense energy you released. This makes you feel lighter and more connected.

Some common adjustment symptoms:

-Getting a cold or flu

-Headaches

-Body aches

-Ear ringing

-Feeling foggy

-Trouble focusing

-Feeling dizzy

Be sure to rest and take it easy as you move through these transitions. It is an important time to nurture yourself after your emotional release.

Step 7: Refocusing Your Energy

A few things happen when you clear negative energy. You will feel lighter and begin to attract better people and opportunities into your life. As you elevate, you are changing your frequency at the core level.

There will also be an adjustment period. It takes some time for your mind to catch up to your emotional shift. As I mentioned earlier I went through two bankruptcies by the time I was 30. These failures left scars in my psyche. Even as better opportunities came in, there was a part of me that did not believe it was happening. At first, it will feel odd to have a positive experience in an area where you struggled in the past.

The more you focus on your desires and creating positive outcomes, the easier it will be. In time, you will come to expect good things in life. Make sure you carve out quiet time each day to connect to your higher self. At higher energy, we are focused on creating something for the greater good, not making money to buy a yacht. Don't get me wrong, there is nothing wrong with buying a yacht if it brings you joy. Issues come up when we become attached to material possessions and status. In this case, the ego is running the show. As you elevate, your higher-self is running the show.

Elevating

What is the first thing you think of when you see a person who is healthy and physically fit? If you are like most, you would assume this person exercises regularly and has a healthy diet.

This next question is designed to shift your perspective:

Is this healthy person doing something or being something?

Yes, these people are doing things like exercising and eating healthy, but it goes beyond the doing. They have become something different. It is not something they have to think about. The same thing happens when you are living in elevated energy. It is not something you do. It is something you become.

One day soon, you will look back and think, *how did I live in that lower state of energy and awareness for so long?* Don't be hard on yourself. This is all part of your journey to deeper discovery.

Enjoy your empowerment and be aware of that tricky ego. It will slide in when you least expect and try to knock you off track. Remain grounded in your spirit and always focus on the greater good. You are walking the line between higher awareness and the physical world. Helping others is beautiful, but not at your own expense. Remain balanced and consistent with your spiritual practice. Thank you for being a light and a blessing to the world.

***

To contact Joe:

Main Site: http://JoeNunz.com

Free webinar: http://freelifeschool.com

You Tube Channel: http://ashotofjoe.com

Membership: http://highergoundnow.com

Elevate Your Energy home study course
http://elevateyourenergynow.com

Jake Cortez

Jake Cortez an Investor, with mastery in Sales, Leadership, & Communication, all byproducts of his pursuit to master the art of public speaking.

Fluent in the language of love, born into this world with four generations of women to welcome him, in addition to his grandmother on his father's side.

Raised in Miami Florida by a single very loving mother, he started working at 15 years old pushing shopping carts.

Over two decades worth of sales experience from cold calling to knocking on well over 10,000 doors. Of his many accomplishments, amplified Streamline pre-merger with Grant Cardone.

Grew his Real Estate Investment portfolio to over 1000 acres in less than a year in 2021. Founding member of an NFT movement where impact, contribution, & art are at its core in his hometown Miami, Florida.

Having an eclectic blend of life experiences has afforded him a unique ability to cultivate a people first orientation to solving challenges. In his limited spare time, he speaks weekly in prisons to support youth in breaking the cycle of recidivism.

Impact is his currency.

A Vision Gives Pain A Purpose

By Jake Cortez

In my self-development journey, I am the hunter, seeking to understand my shadows so that I may develop a deeper understanding of myself, life, and people in general. In my business journey, I have built a brand of achieving results, living with integrity, and profiting intelligently. Through these values, I became the hunted. I began to move in alignment with the beliefs I had regarding my values, and this became my true north. It wasn't always this way; there was a time when I sought to develop the skills I have since attained, which led me to opportunities that fit the profile of my goals.

If you do not decide on what you are seeking or would like to create, life will provide you, by default, what you have floating around in your subconscious.

My voyage of healing began at the ripe age of eighteen years old. About to be released from jail on house arrest, I was faced with a choice after tiring from the repercussions of ill-conceived decisions. I refused to accept this plea bargain, and asked for jail time or freedom, but nothing in between. They kept me in jail. I had been dodging bullets, never doing any real time up until this point because I learned to protect myself. In these times, it was stay free at any cost.

Yes, healing hurts, but staying the same would have been more painful, so I had one option. The decision was easy. Decide. When I cut off the possibility of failure, success became imminent.

When things got really bad in prison, I played the hypothetical game of ending my life by slitting my wrist and bleeding out in a confinement cell. I realized that I was as far off the beaten track as when I had arrived, and I concluded very quickly that ending my life—to end the suffering I created—was not an option either. It was a cowardly move actually, to end my supposed suffering and create more for my mom and family. "You better man the fuck up" appeared in my internal monologue.

The pain I encountered while seeking my salvation paled in comparison to the agony endured from my darkest of emotions imploding within the recesses of my soul. It ripped my heart, leaving it thrown about like a grocery bag in the wind.

With two feet on the ground, I am now staring fate in the face—the good, the bad, and the indifferent. Bring it all. I'm so ready to evolve.

In the process of sitting with what I created, the recent past was on my heels and I had to learn very quickly that being thrown about externally is an indication that my values were not clearly defined. Regardless of the maladaptive behavioral habits I had formed, I knew in my heart that I am not my behavior. What I had created was a mess due to an absurd amount of unattended internal pain. The inexperienced would focus on a symptom and the eradication of the result, while the cause stems from what is causing this cumbersome manifestation. I know who I am and the service I came to provide but living with my heart wide open took enormous amounts of pain, trust, and, most importantly, healing.

Among seven billion humans, no fingerprint is identical, and neither are our journeys.

What Hurts You, Blesses You

My elaborate plan failed miserably. I was naked with the exception of the uncomfortable shroud that covered my body from the waist down. This cell was bigger than most—a spacious nine by nine—and it was different from all the rest. There was no bed or place for a bed. I would sleep on a dark-green mat on the floor with no cover, just a very durable fire-retardant mat about two inches thick. The door to this cell was different as well, as it was made of plexiglass with quarter-inch thick bars running up, down, and across.

The only other things in this cell were a translucent window that allowed sunlight in, but that you could not see out of, and a stainless-steel toilet with a sink. In prison, this cell is referred to as an SOS cell. Anyone who is classified as suicidal will be housed in an SOS cell if deemed necessary.

I was not suicidal, but I did cut my wrist intentionally.

I was being housed in a youth prison called Lancaster Correctional and I hated the place. I had been there for seven days, and on my fifth day I got into a fight over a cookie. Perhaps it wasn't quite a fight—let's just say food and sleep are two things that I rarely lose fights over. The officers were mean white supremacists from the backwoods of Trenton, Florida. There were sixty inmates, ages sixteen to twenty-four, per dorm, and all were required to march everywhere.

Physical training began at 5:30 am every morning. I told the officer that it was the Sabbath and that I could not work out for that reason. He grabbed the hat on my head, threw it on the ground, and said, "Fuck the Sabbath. Get in line."

"I guess I'm training this morning," I thought.

All of these reasons led me to begin thinking that there had to be a way out of there. Mind you, I was eleven months into a twenty-four-month sentence, and when I say "a way out of there," I did not mean "breakout." Rather, I meant transferred to a different prison.

I began my research alongside my fellow inmates. In the process, I met Billy Joe, who had the best idea I had heard thus far, or so I thought.

"If you are suicidal, they have to ship you out of here," he said.

That was all I needed to hear, so I devised a plan. We were required to be clean-shaven every day, so I broke the razor we were issued, took the razor from the shaving apparatus, and sat on the floor by my bunk.

These were open-bay dorms with up to sixty inmates. Bunk beds lined the walls with single bunks in the middle of the room.

I really did not want to die—at least not in that moment in time—so I enlisted the assistance of my comrade Alejandro who just so happened to be my cellmate in the last prison we were in.

I asked him to hold a piece of my skin on my left arm and pull. He did. I pulled out the razor and he jumped as if he had arachnophobia and had just seen the largest spider in the world.

Alejandro was fired from his role in my suicide attempt. Since I really did not want to die, I wanted to avoid cutting a vein. So, I decided to use Alejandro for something else. "When I say go, head to the officer station and tell em that I'm trying to kill myself," I said.

I backed myself all the way up to the wall, seated on the floor, as we were required to do. We were not permitted to sit on our bunks or anything other than the floor until 9:00 pm.

There was a lot of commotion in the dorm as there always was, with people paying attention to their own conversations.

Mentally, I had committed myself to getting out, so in that moment I made the first cut on my wrist. Granted, I cut on an existing scar, actually killing myself would be horrendous, but having another scar is pretty bad as well.

This cutting stuff was not easy. I could see my veins. There was a little blood, but it was not dripping or anything. Nevertheless, it seemed realistic. I told Alejandro, "Go."

He hopped up and began heading to the officer station. I looked down and realized that I wasn't doing this shit right. It looked like I was playing with a kitten.

I saw an officer exit the officer station, moving at a brisk pace. The dorms were pretty large, so I had time, but not much.

At that moment, I began feverishly attempting to make this kitten scratch look believable. The razor was dull because I had extracted it by putting the Bic single-use razor on the ground and stomping it with my boot. This butter knife of a razor was screwing up my plan. I was now cutting like Dana Carvey sings of chopping Broccoli.

The officer was twenty-five feet away moving briskly with his elongated legs. He stood 6' 3" and his legs looked as tall as my body as I glanced up at him from my disempowered suicidal state.

"Inmate COR-tezz drop the razor."

Would a suicidal person drop the razor? Nope. I sliced again for good measure, to hopefully turn this kitten scratch into something somewhat believable.

The dorm went dead silent with the exception of the officer. He raised the decibel level of his request, and this time he started getting angry. Finally, I dropped the razor. The room was so silent and the energy in the room was so dense that you could cut it with a Bic razor—definitely not the one I dropped, however. The sound of the razor hitting the ground was audible, and I was immediately picked up by the collar of my shirt, dragged to the officer station, and put into handcuffs.

The other officer in the booth asked me what was wrong. In full Oscar-nominee mode, I replied with, "Uncle died. I don't want to live anymore."

Escorted to the infirmary, they asked me the same question. I gave them the same answer. They then asked me to strip. At this point, I was accustomed to disrobing in the presence of others. They handed me a shroud and escorted me to the SOS cell. Thus far, the plan had been going great. No more training, no more marching, and my meals were delivered to the flap in the door. Upon entry into the cell, they locked the door behind me. Thereafter, all of the infirmary's day-to-day operations just carried on as if I wasn't there watching through the plexiglass.

I went to sleep on my dark forest-green mat. The walls and roof were a light pastel green. The whole room was green with the exception of the stainless-steel metal toilet. However, there was no toilet paper. I needed to knock on the window when I was ready to take a shit.

I hadn't quite figured out how I was going to manage my time while there.

With two audible bangs, "chow" had arrived. I walked to the flap to grab my styrofoam tray and take it back to my yoga mat. I love breakfast, and the biscuits were not bad. Of course, they were not great for you, but they certainly were not bad. I finished my meal and put the tray back on the flap.

Training at 5:30 am, marching everywhere all day, and having to sit on the floor in a room with no air conditioning can be draining.

I was catching up on sleep, and meal after meal I was eating everything and putting the tray out. They would open my tray and document what I had eaten every meal. By the third day, I had run out of things to think about. I had already gone through how many women I had slept with, including how many were with condoms and how many were without. I had already thought about everything else that I needed to think about.

Something started to tell me they were not going to ship me anywhere. I had cut my arm, and I was in an SOS cell, under observation.

"Wait a minute," I thought. "Do suicidal people eat?" I had been eating every meal as if I was in the Hilton bed and breakfast! "That's it. Tomorrow I starve," I concluded.

When breakfast finally arrived, I ate the biscuit and drank the milk. Everything else went untouched, and breakfast is my favorite meal. When lunch arrived, I committed to acting like a Vogue Magazine model before a centerfold shoot.

When dinner was on its way, I was unbelievably hungry. "If this food enters the cell, I'm going to devour it like an animal," I thought.

Mind you, in these cells, you were not provided with eating utensils. Instead, you were given a paper cup that was sliced right down the middle so that you could scoop the food.

When the flap opened, I put my hands over the flap and prevented the food from entering the cell. If it did, it would enter my mouth shortly thereafter.

The flap closed, and the food was taken away.

I began pacing and talking to myself in the hopes that they would notice and ship me where the rest of the crazy people were. I had no idea if where I was trying to go would be better than my present situation, but I was fully committed.

I hadn't showered in days, nor had I shaved, because the razor I used to shave my face was what I used to get into this prison purgatory.

Every day was predictable; I would watch shifts change and people come and go. Every morning a psych doctor would pop the flap, bend down, and question me, "How are you feeling today?"

My response was the same old, "Like shit."

Then, he would ask, "What would happen if we let

you back on the compound?" "I would kill

myself," I would reply.

The flap would then close until the following day. There was never a real human connection—just a man doing his job.

The next time the flap popped open, it was 7:00 pm. My next visit was supposed to be in the morning by the psych doctor.

It was a nurse—a kind old woman. She leaned into the flap. This was the first time in a long time that someone treated me like a human. She calmly asked, "What's wrong?"

I told her my canned responses, but she was not buying it.

I will never forget her maternal wisdom knowing what would be the chink in my armor. She followed up, "What would your mother say if she saw you like this?"

My knees became weak. I hadn't shaved in days, and I had no clothes except this shroud covering the lower half of my body. I didn't say anything—I couldn't. I had an apple in my throat knowing that this would kill my mother. She would literally start bawling.

This angel of a woman then said, "C'mon, why don't you eat this food? I will heat it up for you." "Ok!" She didn't have to twist my arm, I was starving.

I ate dinner on my yoga mat and was planning my conversation with the doctor the following morning.

Then the flap popped open, and I was asked, "How are you feeling?"

"Well, I had a change of heart. I'm feeling much better," I replied.

I was released that day back to the open population, all because this angel of a lady had brought humanity to an environment in which being cold and detached is part of the job description.

At this point, you are probably thinking, "This is nuts. This guy definitely lost his marbles." At the time it seemed like a damn good idea.

What must happen for one to end up in a situation in which faking suicide seems like a good idea? And be happy in a solitary confinement cell, with or without clothes? What type of violence would cause such an event? How much mental and physical abuse from correctional officers must take place for one to believe that slicing their wrist is a better option?

I grew up pretty normal. I was hyperactive, yes, but I was not a criminal until I started committing crimes. Even then, I am not my behavior. I am a human being whose pain was manifesting itself in very harmful ways. Violence just so happened to be one of those ways. Have you ever been so hurt by someone you loved so dearly? Your mother? Your partner? Your father?

When my father decided to leave my mother, he sat me down on the couch and said "Son, it's not working with me and your mother. We are getting separated. You are now the man of the house," I was eleven years old, and I felt the deepest sense of betrayal one could ever experience. It was a cut so deep that I wanted to make sure no one could cut me like that again. I hated my father for leaving; between the ages of eleven and eighteen, hatred and resentment became the foundations of the cell that incarcerated my soul long before I was in prison. The irony lies in my physical incarceration leading to my spiritual liberation. This is not about prison, and it's not about doing time. Rather, this is about how our choices intensify trauma and exacerbate situations. This is about the mental prison of turning inevitable pain into enduring suffering if not addressed. It is about what had to happen for me to truly be free of the mental prison I had created for myself as a result of pain that I did not know how to manage. The blessing for me has been to recognize any form of prison because how do you free yourself from a mental, relational, business prison if you do not know you are in one?

Stand Guard of the Door of Your Mind

Universal laws that are used to enslave undirected conscious thought can be used to liberate and assist in the proliferation of oneness.

Oneness is just knowing, deep in the belly, that everything is connected. I hurt you, and I hurt me.

Writing about my time in prison is like speaking of a life lived long ago. It almost feels like a different lifetime—one in which the limits of my consciousness had met the threshold of my understanding. All of the external programming I was inadvertently agreeing to, and the terms and conditions of the mental, spiritual, and energetic contracts I was entering into, was the programming I accepted. I had uploaded malware that permeated my conscious mind, which eventually made it to my subconscious. Thereafter, the music that my subconscious started to play was not remotely close to what I wanted to manifest. Traversing Hell, I discovered the pathway to Heaven, in the most gorgeously traumatic of ways.

You may be thinking, "What does all of this have to do with entrepreneurship and life in business?"

I have learned over time that a wise entrepreneur allows nothing to control them—not even their own emotions. Just remember that the gifts we sometimes need don't arrive in the packages we desire. Although prison sucked, it was a necessary part of my evolutionary path. Admitted to two rehabs before the age of eighteen, and on my way to prison for my third time at twenty-four years old—for a total of seven and a half years—I was blessed to hear the voice of God in my solitude.

I became enamored with the ability to bring dreams to life by focusing on the values and habits that allow those things to come forth. This book you are holding in your hands is endorsed by Tony Robbins, and in 2008 while doing time in Moorehaven Correctional Center, I bought Tony Robbins' book *Awakening the Giant Within* with a pack of cigarettes from another inmate. Upon purchasing that book, I had a mission to find a role model worth emulating. I had read books on Warren Buffet, Charlie Munger, Peter Lynch, Bill Gates, and Mark Cuban, and none of them resonated with me like Tony Robbins.

Tony inspired me as a young male to pursue my dreams with a relentless fervor. He gave me the hope to know that what I sought was possible. The book has you outline your business goals, adventure goals, and contribution goals. I have achieved all of those with the exception of a few. One of those goals was to master the art of public speaking. Fortunately, they brought in the group Toastmasters prior to my release from prison, and I had the beautiful opportunity to see how a strong enough "why" could manifest the "how." Never seeking out a Tedx Talk, I did one in November 2018. I implore you to dream and make them wildly beautiful. See all of the colors and feel all the feelings. Hold them in your heart and know they are yours, and they shall be.

"Jake to the podium. You are going to speak on the use of the bayonet in the Civil War. Go." As I dove off into my impromptu speech, I was filled with enchantment as I was consciously co-creating my reality with God. This was all the result of inspired action. It is my life's mission to lead with love and carry the torch of inspiration into my family life, the world of business, my relationships, and the prisons in which I speak. I donate my time and refine the lessons God blessed me with by sharing them with incarcerated youths weekly here in South Florida. I seek to inspire and be inspired.

Lean into the power of inspired action, and watch your dreams unfold with grace.

***

To Contact Jake:

Facebook

https://www.facebook.com/jakecortezzz

Instagram

https://www.instagram.com/thejakecortez

Linkedin

https://www.linkedin.com/in/jakecortez

Email:

thejakecortez@gmail.com

Joshua I. Gorra

Josh Gorra grew up in Lawrence, Ma & resides in RI with his family. He's passionate about maximizing his "time value of life" mindset merging both our personal and professional lives, while tailoring it to the organization. He loves teaching all entrepreneurs his 10 principal mindset and empowering you to find your "drive within" because your mindset is the driver to your destination. Based on overcoming his own obstacles, his greatest gratification is paying it forward & changing one life at a time.

Josh is a national speaker, a best-selling author in Spanish & English & his mission is to transform the work-life balance. He believes his method of work-life integration is going to revolutionize the corporations of today. Running multiple companies, Josh fully understands & appreciates what it takes to accomplish daily wins in both our personal & professional lives. In order to become successful while being fulfilled in the process, we must begin each day with GRATITUDE. Becoming an entrepreneur can be overwhelming but it doesn't have to be if we focus on one day at time.

LET'S FOCUS ON PROGRESS, NOT PROGRESSION!

Maximize EACH Day by Living Each Day to its Full Capacity

By Joshua I. Gorra

<u>Maximize EACH day by living each day to its full capacity</u>

My whole life has been a journey of victories, lessons & losses. My mission is to empower as many entrepreneurs as possible to live without attaching outcome! To have an abundant mindset, be present in the process and trust your journey.

Inevitably many people work in organizations where the bottom line is revenue & nothing else matters. Personally, after working so many odd jobs, opportunities to make a living etc., I realized at an early age many people simply worked where they did out of convenience. It was all they knew; it was an old paradigm given to them and that's what they followed a similar path.

I'll share with you how I gained perspective at such a young age, which would prepare me with a road map on who I wanted to become.

My first job was delivering newspapers at age 9, I made under $100 per week but to me at that time I thought it was all the money in the world. I figured no other 9-year-old is making this kind of income, going to school, playing sports & helping their parents.

My second job was working at a dry cleaner, 14 years old with two gentlemen. One was Korean & the other co-worker was Dominican, neither one understood each other. There I was making $4.00 per hour no tips & making less than when I was 9. I just knew the hours were long, it was hot all day & both of my co-workers were miserable, but that is all they knew. Then I figured there has got to be a better opportunity, so I started working in produce at Star Market. Where I had the added joy of taking the city bus & see how much people settled in life. You see, all these experiences would shape my life forever, experiences teach us what to avoid. At the time, sitting on the bus for hours per week, I'd wonder how did these other adults end up here? Did they settle, were they saving for something good in life, all those questions constantly made me wonder.

Then I turned sixteen & started driving, now I was really clicking! I was working at 2 jobs, a waiter at a friendly's restaurant and retail at Walgreens as a stock clerk. I remember hearing time & a half pay on Sundays for the first time & said wow! My arduous work is paying off I'd think to myself this is it, I'm on my way. After stocking shelves all week, cashier work, & waiting on tables I realized I was working harder not smarter. Why though, why I was wired to work the way I did? My parents worked in factories, we never had enough money for anything growing up, so I associated long hours at work, I will be successful. However, as all the other jobs prior had shown me, people settled, parents settled & I for one was not having that. So, I asked myself a question from that moment on, "how do I make more by the hour, how can I make the most income and still work less?"

Understand I love to work but I also love to spend time with the people I love, so in order to do that we must be efficient with our time. We must be intentional with our time in order to be fully present in all aspects of our life. We can have everything we want if we are clear, concise and confident in how we communicate to ourselves. Then there is the universe, we must also be crystal clear with our energy, our communication & take massive action towards our personal & professional goals.

It wasn't until I started building confidence in different sales positions, speaking to customers, learning the art of selling. I've come to learn; it's not selling once people have decided they want to do business with you. Circuit city gave me that opportunity, where I averaged $34 per hour working in part time. Once you have awareness around time & the best use of time, it is nearly impossible to waste any time because it is the simple most important commodity we have. One day in 2000 when I moved to Rhode Island for college, where I attended Johnson & Wales University, I was on my way to meet someone for coffee when suddenly they were late. I was able to spend some time at a Barnes & Noble's bookstore and came across the first book I would read by Jim Rohn. Now, I could not tell you the name of the girl I was supposed to meet because I don't remember but I will share with you I never forgot the name of that book. It's called, "The Seasons of life," that book changed my perspective on life forever. Nevertheless, I read more of Jim Rohn's books, now I listen on audible and share his philosophy with others who seek guidance on personal development.

I later went on to graduate college with a degree in financial services management & ironically that is the business I've been in since 2004. I realized I can make an impact on people's lives & be compensated for creating solutions to people's problems, their obstacles financially & empowering them to plan for their future.

Then…2015 happened, my first daughter was born, Sofia. I cannot fully describe how I felt but I knew I would no longer be the same man I was. I was overwhelmed with joy, excitement, scared of the future, would I be a good father, all these thoughts running through my mind constantly. My DNA in these life changing moments was to remain busy, so I dove into my business & real estate to provide for my family. Then in 2017 Vanessa & I welcomed our second daughter Madeline, now the pressure was really pouring on. I had a little family, everyone depended on me to succeed. I took on those responsibilities and nearly collapsed because without a plan, life can be overwhelming. I was thirty pounds heavier, unhealthy, tired all the time, just not happy in many areas of my life. At the same time, my mother's health was getting worse. Needless to say, I needed to develop systems & that is when I was started to develop to become the best version of myself. I am still not there, I may never get there, but my pursuit & passion to become better will never end until I die.

Anyhow, I bought and sold eighteen units in real estate as a new investor in the last 6 years, but here is why I did. I believed real estate would provide cash flow, deductions, etc. what I didn't account for was TIME and/or lack of time. How could I manage three hundred clients in financial services, manage eighteen tenants, become a new father, find quality time for my relationship with my fiancé, find time to exercise, the list went on & on. Yes, I had multiple property owners & an assistant, but it was still undeniably a ton of work for one person. Unless you have systems, where you can delegate & automate. Hindsight is always 2020, however now I implement what I have learned, at 39 I can certainly say I am much wiser than I was at 33, life lessons are the best teacher. Failure is not a loss when we take what we learned & turn those lessons into victories, write that down.

The root of all happiness lies within systems & how well we can delegate as well as automate items in our life that waste precious time. I now use CRM's, newsletters, I also have a staff that consists of an office manager, a relationship manager, and virtual assistants as needed. Money will not make anyone change; it only brings out the true character we have inside. When we are grounded, confident in who we are and clear around our PURPOSE, we become almost invincible. I can wholeheartedly tell you that more income is wonderful, but it will not change how you feel when you miss bedtime with your children. If you are overweight the convertible won't change your disgust for how you feel. It will not change how you think of other places & people you are supposed to be around but cannot be because you decided to take another meeting. I've been there, I know exactly how it feels & the loss of time never gets replenished. Anyone who tells you differently does not understand work-life integration, nor do they understand this lesson until much later in life, when its too late. When we make our family a priority, when we make our health a priority, when we choose faith over fear…that's when life changes for us. That is when we evolve & we start to appreciate all the little wonders of life. Just waking up in the morning is blessing, spending time with our children is blessing, being able to breath is a blessing! Perspective is earned not given; therefore, I implore you to share your experiences with as many people as possible once you have gained this level of gratitude. Once you have it is not enough to do more for ourselves, we must pay it forward & help others who have not reached this level of freedom.

Here is what changed for me, I started getting up at 5am & started keeping a journal of how I felt each day but began EACH day by writing two people I'm thankful for. Then it morphed into let's add two experiences from the day before that I'm equally thankful for. I also complete 45-90 mins of exercise 5 days per week & drink more water throughout the day. I care more about my health now then I ever did in the past. Then once I was comfortable with 5am I moved my wake-up time to 4am because I did not want to miss breakfast in the mornings with my family nor did I want to miss my workout. I used to go to a local gym that would take me 30 round trip just driving there and coming home each morning. To shave more time in my morning routine I built a gym at home that consists of a Peloton treadmill, a bench, an elliptical & some free weights. Nothing fancy, just something I could get up and go downstairs to begin each day. Guess what, it works! I have more energy throughout the day when I exercise compared to when I don't. When I consume at least a gallon of water per day I eat healthier and consume less food. I also only eat fruit in the morning until noon at least five out of the seven days because I read a book called "fit for life" by Harvey Diamond. By implementing this simple step in my morning, it helps your system process food more efficiently and extends your lifespan while decreasing health issues, so I figured why not. It also saves me a tremendous amount of time to make breakfast for myself & my family. I love when the entire house is sleeping & I've been awake for 2 hours, completed my exercise regimen, then going to start working on breakfast for my girls & my lady. The other system I implemented is, I enrolled Vanessa into my morning workout mindset. She now loves to get up at 5am to jumpstart her day with an excellent work out as well. It was not always like that, when I met her over nine years ago waking up before 9:00 o'clock was not her favorite part of Saturday. I've never met anyone who adores her sleep more than Vanessa but now, she's my accountability partner. On mornings when I'm tired or I went to bed late, she nudges me to wake up to begin our morning routine.

Most people focus on winning the macro-goal, the long-term vision but hardly ever do we see folks focus on their micro-goals. Once I noticed a change in my overall life, routines, success & impact I was making at work, I wanted to apply the same tenacity to my personal life. How can I be more present, really listen with intention when my family speaks to me? It dawned on me that we need to be the same person at home as we are at work because that is how we practice & practice makes progress. It provided me with an awareness that from now on at work I would be present in each meeting, if I were driving, I was intentional about listening to audible books and learning a new craft or listening to an inspiring biography. I started to view every day as an opportunity to maximize each day or as I refer to "max out" to its full capacity. I do not like to waste time; it feels like the worst loss of capital once we truly begin to appreciate how finite we all really are.

My message is this, focus on being happy from within. Nothing external can provide us with the genuine happiness we seek. The money you make is temporary, the cars we drive are temporary, our life which is priceless is temporary. We all forget that someday we all die, how we choose to live our lives while we are alive is what truly is special. If you find yourself not feeling fulfilled with a particular Job that you drive an overly priced vehicle to, it is time to reassess & change direction. This is precisely why I launched my coaching business, Destination Driven LLC & love collaborating with companies who need to enhance their culture. When a corporation loses culture, they lose morale, then they lose the workforce. I empower organizations utilizing my 6-week course where we identify what needs to be amended. We assess what is working & double down on those traits. We provide a blueprint to function with a mindset of abundance not scarcity. My free on-line workbook will help you become aware of what you would like to work on & by the end of the exercise you will realize that you would like to work together, or we part as friends.

The focus is always PROGRESS not perfection. Today being a great father to my children supersedes everything else. I share with my family all the time, you take care of you & I'll take care of me, that way we give each other the best version of ourselves. For my daughters to have that level of self-awareness at 6 & 4 years old, it's powerful. They are fully onboard & responsible for giving each day everything they have, being present in all situations, give more than you take regardless of the encounter.

When we look at ourselves in the mirror, what questions come to mind? Are we where we want to go or do we have some work to do? Do I blame others for my success or my failure? These are all questions that are built into our mindset of "You vs You." I will help you establish accountability around yourself & not point fingers at anyone but yourself daily. This also will remove the inefficiency of comparison to others, remember #MINDSET is everything.

If you own a company that has 1-50 employees, consider this. It is always less expensive to retain happy employees then constantly hire & fire people. When you implement these 10 principles you will have your checklist and ready to win every day.

Utilize these 10 principles daily to create a lifestyle in 90 days:

- Gratitude
- Self-Care
- Passion
- Circle of Influence
- Learn
- Trust your Journey
- Giveback
- Discipline yourself (you vs you)
- Mentoring
- Inspire someone & be inspired

Visit JoshGorra.com for context on each principle & to order a copy of my international best-selling book, "Change your mindset, change your future." You can also find us on Twitter @GorraJoshua, Instagram @JoshGorra & Facebook @JoshuaGorra.

I wish you all health, happiness & success in this game called LIFE. In order to reach new heights, we must choose what direction we want to go to, we must never leave anything to chance! If my story inspired you, please send it to a co-worker, friend or family member who would benefit from a shift in perspective.

***

To contact Josh:
www.JoshGorra.com
@JoshGorra on Instagram
@GorraJoshua on twitter
@JoshuaGorra on FB
1 Marina Park Dr. Suite 1410
Boston, MA 02210

Milan Milosevic

Co-Founder of Riches and Beyond, Founder of Millionaire Speakers, host of Riches and Beyond and a Millionaire Speakers podcast, Editor in Chief of Millionaire Speakers Magazine, International speaker, entrepreneur, speakers coach, and a property mentor.

Milan left his country Serbia 15 years ago as a college dropout who could barely speak English. Over time he was mentored by top property investors and speakers.

After seeing massive success in the property investment business, Milan co-founded Riches and Beyond, a leading South African Property education company with now over 45,000 students and a powerful program that transformed the lives of aspiring and seasoned property investors. Milan is also the founder of the Millionaire Speakers program which teaches how to build a business to 7 figures with your story and speaking. Being an international speaker for over 15 years and having done over 1,000 live presentations as well as hundreds of webinars, he learned from the greats like Robert Kiyosaki, Les Brown, Lisa Nichols, Jim Francis, Bob Proctor, Michel Beckwith and spoken in the US, UK, Dubai, and South Africa!

Featured in Your Business Magazine, Entrepreneur Magazine, Powerhouse Speakers, and several business podcasts as a regular guest expert. Milan is passionate about transferring knowledge to others and empowering aspiring entrepreneurs.

"The true secret in business is in building relationships and providing enormous value." - Milan Milosevic

How Did the College Dropout Who Couldn't Speak English Become 8 Figure Speaker?

By Milan Milosevic

Another event is done.

Comments are coming in the webinar chat:

"Thank you, Milan for your knowledge and expertise!"

"Thank you for this inspiring presentation!"

"Thank you Milan for sharing your passion and transforming lives with education!"

"Milan, you are the best speaker ever!"

A smile overtakes my face.

One-click on the End Webinar button and the event is over.

Disconnecting all the cables, closing the laptop and putting it away, packing the mic carefully in the case. Having a last sip of the remaining energy drink.

It's already 8 pm.

Ready to go home to my kids, they have been waiting for me all day. Couldn't come sooner, Masterclass planning, Webinar setup, team meetings, 30 staff members, 45,000 students, several successful programs and I am in the middle of it…business doesn't wait.

Maserati Granturismo is waiting at the office parking with my name on it. Key switch and the beast revvs loudly. YES! That's why I bought it, reminded me of me. Beautiful navy matte color, silent when wants to be but loud when angry. Music plays my favorite song: "Danza Kuduro!" Kids love it as well. Dark South African night, empty road, heading home.

Thoughts are bringing back the memories. How did I end up here?

Most people know me as Milan, Co-Founder of Riches and Beyond, Founder of Millionaire Speakers, property investor, mentor, and a powerful speaker who shared the stage with Robert Kiyosaki, Les

Brown, Lisa Nichols. Milan who drives a Maserati lives in the big house and travelled to the Maldives and 40 other countries. The man who spoke internationally and changed the lives of over 45,000 people.

People say Milan, we want to be like you.

Many people don't know that 16 years ago I was a broke college dropout who could barely speak English. Born and raised in Serbia, a small European country with friendly people and wonderful nature.

My dad was an electrician, a modest man who taught me morals and family values.

He was not an entrepreneur but always had a piece of good advice. All advice was directed to education. So, I listened to my dad and ended up in college. First-year started working at the same time…stretched somehow to the second year and it was inevitable. Just couldn't study and work so I dropped out of college.

Work made me happy even with the little salary I had, but I finally felt useful. I was contributing to the family. WE were going thru some rough times financially. Even my dad in his retirement had to continue working part-time as an electrician to bring food to the table. Years went by and I changed different jobs. Every new one was better paid but it was not enough. I did learn from my dad that the secret to wealth was to save. After 4 years of working, I saved enough and managed to buy myself a second-hand car. White 4 door Fiat Uno! It was beautiful!

Now that I am thinking it was a piece of junk but hey, my first car and my hard work paid for it. Youngsters only want to have a car and to have fun. I was no exception. All saved money went into that car.

Interestingly enough I started realizing something that will set my mindset in a different direction.

Questions started raising. Am I going to work for 4 more years and perhaps buy myself a Fiat Punto which was a car model after? Didn't like the idea of working for second-hand cars for so many years and still being broke at the end.

Somehow didn't make sense and the great advice I got from my dad electrician was:

"Milan, if you want to make more money get the better-paid job!" So, I started changing jobs.

From selling lavender from door to door and many no's and doors slapped in my face to working in the shoe store selling Italian high-quality shoes. Still know all about the shoes and can tell from a mile away the foot size.

It was a great experience but somehow It was not enough. I felt deep inside of me that there are more, more opportunities somewhere else and that I have to find that place and follow my heart, or I will never be happy if I don't do that.

I applied for different jobs locally and internationally and got the offer. 12. August 2005 was the day when I left my country Serbia to go and work in America on a cruise ship. I was standing at the airport with my dad and he started getting emotional. "Milan, let's go back home. Got to be another way. Do you know that people leave our country and never come back?" Great man, wanted to keep his family together.

I grabbed my dad's hands and said, "Dad I have to do this. I don't fit here anymore.

But I promise you, one day I will make you proud!" And that was the moment I left.

As the plane was taking off, I looked at my country Serbia last time 16 years ago and all I was thinking was what am I leaving behind. Everything and everybody I ever loved. My friends and family.

The real question is Are you willing? Are you willing to leave everything behind, everything that was ever holding you back to go and pursue your own greatness? If you are willing, success will come!

I could barely speak English. How, yes, no that was me. Pretty basic level but one thing I had all my life and that was stubborn willingness to go after I want, no matter what.

Long story short I worked on the cruise ship for 10 years. Met my wife, an African lady from South Africa, and eventually, we got married. Together we have changed different positions that the cruise ship industry allowed. From casino dealers' positions and gift shops to art auctioneers and future cruise experts. I always like to say that you are not looking for your passion, your passion will find you.

I saw a speaker once on the ship. He was an American speaker. He was brilliant. Somehow deep inside I knew that this is what I was meant to do. Challenge was I had a bad Serbian accent but again with a burning desire to succeed.

It was a journey of growth, and I am grateful for that opportunity. Those were the best years of my life.

10 years after working on the cruise ship we have decided to settle down in South Africa. We had some money saved and started investing in real estate. We tried to do it our own way but didn't really work out according to the plan.

In 2014, we started investing in personal development and different mentors and this is when our lives changed for the better. Mindset and being open to the right knowledge. Our first multimillionaire mentor taught us valuable lessons and after seeing success in our lives, we started teaching our friends and family. They started seeing success. Eventually, we started the company called Riches and Beyond, and now years later with over 45,000 students and over $50 million raised for our student's deals. I am sharing this story to say that it is possible with enough commitment, dedication, perseverance, and a little bit of passion. We have our own TV Show, The Property Game on The Home Channel where our students share their stories and strategies. These are our students who were beginners and now doing deals. Also, people who had few properties and now they have multiplied them. There are also our students who have done 7 deals in 6 months and some of them manage to own their own property development and block of flats in less than two years. The most beautiful part is they didn't have any of their own money.

We have learned from the best and now we are able to teach others how to do the same.

As we speak, my business partners and I are busy building our first hotel and a massive $100 million project.

Maserati revvs again and head into the night.

100 million…a thought went thru my head while passing thru the night. How could this guy, who was a college dropout, who could barely speak English, who was broke and didn't know anyone here manage to do something like this?

The simple lesson is this: Does not matter where are you coming from, what matters is where are you heading. Clarity will take you to success. Stay long enough on the path and eventually you will see success. It is inevitable!

So how did I end up here? Driving my dream car, living in a dream house, changing lives every day?

Passion will find you eventually.

Yes, I love real estate, but I love speaking more. Somehow, speaking became part of me.

16 years later after leaving my country Serbia and after more than 1,000 live events, hundreds of webinars, seminars, presentations and keynotes I realized that speaking is something I would do even if I don't get paid.

Somebody said a long time ago: *"Find something you are passionate about and you will never work for the rest of your life!"*

I was honored and privileged to learn from the greats like Lisa Nichols, Les Brown, Michael Beckwith, Bob Proctor, Robert Kiyosaki, Lewis Howes and Toni Robbins. With some of these people, I have even shared the stage and some of them like Lisa Nichols became my close coaches and guides.

After speaking in many countries such as the US, UK, Dubai, South Africa Live and virtually, and after many requests to train others, my passion has found me again.

This is how the Millionaire Speakers program was born.

What if your story can change lives? What if while you are on that stage sharing your story and an idea, there is a little kid listening. A little kid who might have been bullied, with no hope for the future.

And what if your story can give him hope. What if that kid one day becomes a president, a world-class leader who will change the lives of many because of you. Because your story did something to him and showed him that it is possible.

Yes, your story can potentially change lives and inspire others, but it does require courage. Courage to be brave to share it, own it, and turn it into your superpower. Then and only then when you own your story, you will win your life and be ready to change others.

The Millionaire Speakers program is about your story but also building a business to 7 and 8 figures with your story. I have done it; my students have done it and you can do the same thing.

Speaking on the stage should be a by-product and a front end for your product or service. But before you go into business, you need to know who you are and what do you stand for. This is where your story comes into place.

There are always 3 things needed in order to grow business to 8 figures. Your story, marketing, and business structure.

Being in business for 16 years I learned that a lot of companies don't get this right.

There might be a great story behind their product/service but there is no marketing or a business structure. Or they can have a story and marketing but no idea how to get clients. Or Great marketing and business but no personality. We are living in the age of building long-term relationships and the only way to do that is with a willingness to be who you are, and this way attract the client who is like you. This way becomes a natural transition from curiosity to likeness to a lifetime client.

This approach has been proven with all our and our students' brands. There is always a story and a personal touch behind the brands. Combined with the powerful marketing and excellent customer service and structure, this becomes a natural win-win situation.

Maserati revvs again as it went up the gear.

I remember the first time I cried with Lisa Nichols on the stage in front of thousands.

3,000 people heard my story. As I was heading off the stage there were men, strong men came to me and said; *"Thank you Milan! I went thru the same thing! Thank you for reminding me how powerful I am. Thank you for being strong for all of us. Thank you for inspiring us. Thank you!"* They said that to me, a broke college dropout who couldn't speak English.

But wait, I am no longer that guy. I have grown, I am not the same person. I spoke in front of thousands, my students have built massive companies, wrote bestselling books, my students are powerful keynote speakers, my students are powerful CEO's and every single one of them has a powerful story.

I am not the same guy anymore, I am better. Somebody said to me: "Milan, you have changed."

My response: "We have to!"

Maserati slowed down, enter the garage of a beautiful contemporary house in a quiet upmarket Johannesburg neighborhood.

The door opened up and two 5-year-old kids, twins, a boy, and a girl started running from a house door. "Daddy, Daddy! Did you change lives? Did you buy some chocolate?"

Somehow, they always know what to ask to make me smile. Both answers are of course YES!

In the end, nothing matters if you are not happy. There are never enough people who need help and there is never enough satisfaction in seeing them succeed.

Today I am a founder of the Millionaire Speakers program, a program that changes lives and helps entrepreneurs share their stories and grow their business to 7 and 8 figures. I am in the media, TV, magazines, radio stations and business podcasts. My students are celebrities and CEOs as well as regular people. Every single one of them has a powerful story to share and inspire. I am a coach who helps them find themselves in their story. The story is there to inspire but also to remind us that without the story we won't be here where we are today. Our story brought us to this point and everything we are going thru today is preparing us for the future.

I am still the same person inside but with different, more advanced skill sets. Yes, I have failed many times but never gave up on my dreams. Every time I failed, I failed forward. Learned the lesson and kept moving forward.

In small groups, I am usually the quietest person but on the other end, I can speak in front of thousands. I learned that it is not who you are but what you do that defines you and I also learned that nothing is impossible. If someone else were able to do it, you can do the same thing.

My story is here to inspire you and to remind you that not so long ago there was a little kid from Serbia, who didn't know what to do with his life, couldn't speak English, and had no money.

While most people quit on their dreams, this one quit on things that were not serving him.

This one took a leap of faith, gave his best effort to become the best version of himself, learned from the best, shook hands with the greats, and one day indeed he made his dad proud.

"Dreams were never given to you without the possibility of becoming a reality!"

***

-Milan Milosevic

To contact Milan:

www.millionairespeakers.com

https://www.facebook.com/millionairespeakers

milan@richesandbeyond.com

contact number:

+27 10 109 3402

Afterword

Life and business are always a series of transitions… people, places, and things that shape who we are as individuals. Often, you never know that the next catalyst for improving your business and life is around the corner, in the next person you meet, next mentor you hire or the next book you read.

Jim Britt and Kevin Harrington have spent decades influencing individuals and entrepreneurs with strategies to grow their business, developing the right mindset and mental toughness to thrive in today's business environment and to live a better life.

Allow all you have read in this book to create a new you, to reinvent yourself and your business model if required, because every business and life level requires a different you. It is your journey to craft.

Cracking the Rich Code is a series that offers much more than a book. It is a community of like-minded influencers from around the world. A global movement. Each chapter is like opening a surprise gift, that just may contain the one idea that changes everything for you. Watch for future releases and add them to your collection. If you know of anyone who would like to be considered as a co-author for a future volume, have them email our offices at support@jimbritt.com

The individual and combined works of Jim Britt and Kevin Harrington have filled seminar rooms to maximum capacity and created a worldwide demand. If you get the opportunity to attend one of their live events, jump at the chance. You'll be glad you did.

If you are a coach, speaker, consultant of entrepreneur and would like to get the details about becoming a coauthor in the next Cracking the Rich Code book in the series, contact Jim Britt at support@jimbritt.com or watch this video and schedule a time to speak with Jim: https://www.richcode.club/beacoauthor/

STRUGGLING WITH MONEY ISSUES?

Check out Jim's latest program "Cracking the Rich Code" which focuses on the subconscious programs influencing one's financial success, that keeps most living a life of mediocrity. This powerful four-month program is designed to change one's relationship with money and reset your money programming to that of the wealthy. More details at: www.CrackingTheRichCode.com

To Schedule Jim Britt or Kevin Harrington as a featured speaker at your next convention or special event, online or live, email: support@jimbritt.com

Master each moment as they become hours that become days.

Make it a great life!

Your legacy awaits.

STAY IN TOUCH

www.JimBritt.com

www.JimBrittCoaching.com

www.CrackingTheRichCode.com

www.KevinHarrington.tv

www.richcode.club/beacoauthor/

For daily strategies and insights from top coaches,

speakers and entrepreneurs, join us at:

THE RICH CODE CLUB---FREE members community.

www.TheRichCodeClub.com